American Art Jewelry Today

American Art Jewelry Today

Susan Grant Lewin

Forewords by Barbara Rose
Jack Lenor Larsen

Thames and Hudson

This book is dedicated to my mother, May Lipsky Feman, and the memory of her sister, Goldie Lipsky Hoffman, who introduced me to Victorian jewelry in the antique district of Philadelphia. This fascination later grew to encompass and then totally focus on contemporary artists' jewelry. And to Hal, Adam, Gaby, Jeanne, Elias, and Natasia.

Editor: Lory Frankel
Designer: Dirk Luykx

Frontispiece: Robert W. Ebendorf. Necklace. 1985. Japanese rice paper. 24-karat gold foil, lacquer, silver, copper, ebony. Diam. 12″. Collection Victoria & Albert Museum, London. Photograph: A. Chan

First published in Great Britain in 1994 by
Thames and Hudson Ltd, London

Copyright © 1994 Susan Grant Lewin

First published in 1994 by Harry N. Abrams, Incorporated, New York

British Library Cataloguing-in-Publication Data

A catalogue record for this book is available from the British Library

ISBN 0-500-01644-5

Printed and bound in Japan

Contents

Foreword

In his *Autobiography,* Benvenuto Cellini, the acclaimed goldsmith of the Renaissance, lamented the inferior status of the craftsman vis-à-vis the newly elevated position of painters and sculptors. The latter had gained new social status, not to mention high fees, tax benefits, and all manner of desirable "perks" as practitioners of the liberal or "free" forms of fine art. Cellini's success with his dual career as artisan and artist proved there was really no difference in style or subject between his miniature work as a goldsmith and his large-scale sculpture. Not known for modesty, Cellini bragged that his bronze figure of *Perseus* was the most famous sculpture in Italy. The work, which shows Perseus holding the decapitated head of the Gorgon Medusa, an allegory of Medici power, was commissioned as a public sculpture for the town square of Florence. If Cellini wished to discredit the idea of a separation between the arts and crafts, he obviously did not win his case: making objects of use—no matter how beautifully—continued to be considered manual labor rather than an intellectual discipline.

The distinction between art invented by the imagination of the individual "genius" and craft, which followed tradition and precedent and was distinguished qualitatively through workmanship rather than originality, was made by the architect, painter, and theorist Leon Battista Alberti. The separation between manual craft and intellectual art was further promulgated by the artist-inventor Leonardo. Here it is interesting to note that the full-fledged Renaissance "genius" himself focused on inventing technology and armaments. Artisan-artists, who might make useful objects like table settings and adornments, on the other hand, specialized not in the deadly arts of war but in making functional things to enhance the good life. In this connection we may observe that the current interest in jewelry as an art form is occurring in a context of disarmament in civilized countries when a new agenda requires the human intelligence to focus on the quality of life as opposed to inventing new forms of death and destruction.

During the Middle Ages, there was no clear distinction made between craft and art. During the so-called Dark Ages following the collapse of the Roman Empire, the minor arts, especially those associated with the jewelers' techniques of inlay and metalwork, took center stage. The resurrection of classical aesthetics as well as the return of the forms of antiquity in the Renaissance encouraged artists to proclaim themselves intellectuals, philosophers, and gentlemen worthy of considerable remuneration and good dinners at the tables of the rich and famous. Organizing themselves into fine arts academies instead of craft guilds, artists lobbied for and achieved social parity with their patrons, the newly rich merchant humanists. The Medici and other great families, whose fortunes depended on capitalist transactions rather than great intellectual and cultural accomplishments, brought glory to the family name by commissioning public art and large-scale decor for their villas and palaces.

Painters like Titian and Bronzino took care to depict in specific detail the fabulous jewelry of their sitters, but the names of the artisans who created these pieces, which often had special names and became famous in themselves, were by and large forgotten. Workmanship and the rarity of the materials, not the style or name of their makers, determined the value of the rings, necklaces, earrings, tiaras, chains, medallions, pins, bracelets, clasps, and so on. The official portraits of the dukes of Burgundy, for example, identify their subjects as wearing the *Toison d'or,* the solid gold necklace of the Order of the Golden Fleece. We know the names of the Burgundian dukes and of those who painted them, but who remembers the artisan who created the incredible jeweled necklace?

In his classic study of art collecting, *The Rare Art Traditions,* Joseph Alsop identifies what is common to all societies that collect art for its own sake, independent of its use as practical or ritual object. Among the most important considerations is the fame of the creator, which is passed on by art history, thus assuring immortality and continuing material value. Anonymity versus fame is precisely the issue that continues to divide the major from the minor and the fine from the applied arts. Jewelry remains craft so long as the names of individual creators are relatively unknown. The emergence of personal style among jewelers and museum exhibitions of their work are as important for the collecting of jewelry as any other factors one may identify as defining art.

The major obstacle to the identification of jewelry as a legitimate form of contemporary art has a curious origin. When the Museum of Modern Art was set up, new departments were created for the "minor" arts of photography, printmaking, and design. However, it was assumed that modern design was industrial and consequently utilitarian. Traditionally, jewelry has always been status ornamentation. Even if worn by witch doctors, it has no practical utilitarian use. The spoon the witch doctor uses to stir potions may be the ancestor of the streamlined Bauhaus utensil, but his (or her) necklace does not lend itself to standardization. The irony is that the Arts and Crafts movement, in its desire to return to handicraft in reaction to industrialization, began the process of ghettoizing jewelry as an undemocratic *objet de luxe,* socially unacceptable and politically incorrect. Add to this the American prejudice against class-linked ostentation—the only Puritan ornament imaginable is the scarlet letter A—and you realize that only the greatness of native American jewelry could win out over the Puritan and Shaker prohibitions against personal adornment to be exhibited as art in American museums.

We have observed that the rise of the liberal arts paralleled the status strivings of an upwardly mobile entrepreneurial class seeking to replace the hereditary feudal aristocracy. The distinction between the work of the hand and that of the mind is fundamental to the world view of humanism. At the heart of this argument is the superior value placed by philosophers on conceptual cerebration as opposed to manual execution—the Neoplatonic Idea as opposed to its mere reflection in a real and mundane object. This privileging of the major disciplines as the "fine" as opposed to the applied arts, which began in the Renaissance, has endured until today. The essays in this book go a long way in opening the door to a redefinition of contemporary jewelry as art. The collection, preservation, and exhibition of the objects reproduced here and in a growing body of literature on the subject will surely aid in establishing contemporary jewelry as an art form in its own right. Necessary to this reevaluation is the fine balance between the discipline of artisanship and the freedom of individual conception and expression. The loss of skill and discipline in the outer limits of permissiveness of the avant-garde may well encourage a new interest in such discipline-intensive mediums as art jewelry.

Barbara Rose

If Susan Lewin's inquiry raises the question of art jewelry as a too-little-known expression of our time, this book also reopens a floodgate of such conundrums as "What exactly are the defining boundaries of art?"

Even if we concede that art (at least fine art) cannot be useful (currently useful, that is; if it is as old as Han dynasty bronzes, utilitarian crafts *become* art), as art jewelry does not function, it might just qualify. That jewelry hangs on a God-given shoulder, not a painted wall, should not be a serious detractor. Nor should its modest scale—it was Henry Moore who reminded us that the largest *and* smallest forms possess the most power.

That art jewelry has been even more neglected than art glass, ceramic vessels, and tapestry may be because of residual post-Victorian associations with jewelry itself as either conformist and ladylike *or* the baubles and trinkets of gypsies and harlots . . . or the extravagance of dependent women.

If today beclouded by several current and commercial modes and too often valued by the mere weight of materials used, jewelry yet remains a basic and primal art form. Indeed, in most cultures jewelry is mankind's oldest art form, only slightly younger than the first rudimentary tools. Rings, amulets, and beads are found in burials of many preceramic cultures.

Certain jewelry predates by millennia woven textiles, and it was highly developed by many Arctic, African, and island people without either textiles or ceramics. For many of these cultures jewelry was a highly developed art, both in terms of the several skills used in its making and in its power of expression.

Barbara Rose points to the High Renaissance as a time when expressions in craft mediums lost ground to painting and sculpture. Indeed, it was Vasari who created this now passing hierarchy of higher and lower arts. But it was in Europe, too, that jewelry fell into the narrowing range of conventionalized forms familiar today through increasingly repetitive production means. More often shallow symbols of conformity than hallmarks of distinction, these are principally valued for their materials and techniques of manufacture.

In contrast, recall for a moment such magnificent archaic forms as the gold masks of pre-Columbian Peru, or the lightweight crowns of Silla monarchs of medieval Korea—so kinetic as to pick up a dazzling golden light with the slightest movement of the wearer. Or earlier, when polished jade segments were wired as coats of mail for Han dynasty royalty—one of those occasions when jewelry became raiment in its highest form.

By comparison, today's jewelry is—even more than costume—a stripped-down affair, tame by comparison. Medea would have thought so, as would Louis XIV. Of course, jewelers in most of these epochs also had the men's trade!

So, Susan Lewin, high time and well said.

Jack Lenor Larsen

8

Acknowledgments

A project like this usually involves the participation of many people and, although someone's name will be invariably forgotten, I want to extend my thanks to *everyone* who participated in this project.

This book would not have been possible without the invaluable contribution of Thomas Gentille, a man who has quite literally dedicated his life to jewelry, artistic integrity, and the contemporary jewelry movement in the United States. Thomas has been a very special advisor and educator through the process of writing this book, as well as an insightful editor. I am enormously grateful to him. And to Pavel Opocensky who, with Thomas Gentille, helped to formulate and solidify the direction this book would eventually take.

Jack Lenor Larsen and Barbara Rose, undoubtedly two of the busiest people on earth, gave this project their most precious gift—time. With their forewords, they have added another dimension to this book. For this added perspective, I thank them both.

Jo Anne Schlesinger was brilliant in her coordination and administration of all of the many details involved in developing this book. Her contribution was invaluable, and I cannot thank her enough.

I would also like to thank a small group of jewelers and critics who were always there when help was needed: Jamie Bennett, Helen W. Drutt English, Arline Fisch, Lisa Gralnick, Toni Greenbaum, Mary Lee Hu, Dan Jocz, and Charon Kransen. In addition, I would like to extend special thanks to Suzanne Ramljak, editor and art historian, for her critical eye and helpful input. Suzanne's contribution to the text of the portfolio was invaluable. For his contributions to the Glossary and Bibliography, my thanks to Tim McCreight. Thomas Gentille also offered his help with the Glossary.

A special and sad thank you is also extended to the late Vanessa Lynn, who believed so strongly in this movement and contributed so much to this field; she was always generous with her time and knowledge.

Thank you also to Marybeth Shaw, who joined me on my first jewelry expedition, instigated by Mickey Friedman when she was curator of design at the Walker Art Center; it was she who requested that I lend my "eye" to the Walker's jewelry selection. Kay McGuire, also at the Walker at that time, often shared with me the quest for undiscovered talent.

Most of all, I'm appreciative to where it all started—that fateful day in 1983 when Robert Ebendorf and Ivy Ross won "Surface & Ornament II" for their Color-Core jewelry. These two jewelers were the first to educate me to the beauty of artist jewelry using nonprecious materials. The fit with Formica was a natural; hence, "Surface & Edge," an exhibition of art jewelry made with Formica laminate, was born. Thank you as well to the untiring Graham Hughes, who believed in the project enough to bring it to the Edinburgh Festival, and also to Harry Dennis, who encouraged me from the start, and to Jeff Kiser, who gave me a needed push.

Special thanks to Harry N. Abrams's Julia Moore, who believed in the book from the beginning; to my editor, Lory Frankel, for her knowledge, talent, and guidance in helping me get to this finished product; and to Dirk Luykx, whose design added greatly to this collaboration.

Last, but certainly not least, I want to thank my family—Hal, Adam, and Gaby—for their patience and understanding, especially when they must have felt neglected as I devoted long evenings and weekends to this project.

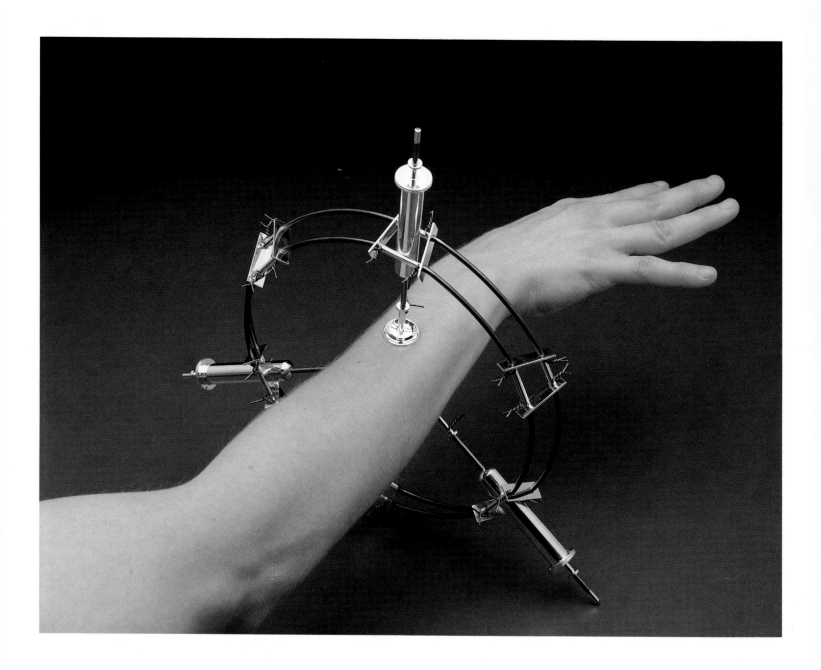

Boris Bally. *Constrictor.* Arm form. 1990.
Sterling silver, three rubies, oxidized brass,
anodized titanium, stainless steel springs.
Fabricated silver, tube settings, cold jointing, rivets, twist joints. 11 x 11 x 2″,
expanding to 12½ x 12½ x 2″. Collection
the artist. Photograph: David L. Smith

Introduction:
American Artists' Jewelry

SUSAN GRANT LEWIN

This book is about an ancient craft transforming itself into a modern art form. While the status and acceptance of jewelry as art have increased over the years, there are still barriers to be broken. The spirited debate among artists in this vibrant and invigorated field continually redefines our relationship to jewelry, and the passion displayed in their work demands that it be given serious consideration as a new genre of artistic expression. On the other hand, art jewelry continues to struggle against a public perception that is shaped by the sanitizing effect of the commercial jewelry industry, which disconnects jewelry from cultural and artistic associations. As a result, jewelry has been misunderstood and overlooked as a legitimate form of artistic expression.

Thomas Gentille, one of the artists featured in this book, describes jewelry's condition well. Likening its struggle for recognition to that of photography, Gentille observed, "Photography is a recent invention, it had birth and rapid growth in a relatively short period of time. Jewelry, on the other hand, has been around for thousands of years along with as many attitudes towards it. It had to break through rigidly defined boundaries."[1]

"Modern Handmade Jewelry," 1946, an exhibition of jewelry made by painters, sculptors, and art jewelers held at New York's Museum of Modern Art, was one of the first major acknowledgments of wearable art as a movement in America. "An important objective of the show, which included 135 pieces, was to bring together the 'artist as jeweler' and 'jeweler as artist,' a concept that had been neglected since the turn of the century."[2] Such renowned artists as Alexander Calder and Jacques Lipchitz were exhibited next to pioneering figures in the studio jewelry movement like Margaret de Patta and Sam Kramer. This event, plus subsequent shows of modern jewelry at the Walker Art Center, Minneapolis, in 1948, 1955, and 1959, indicated the degree of artistic recognition achieved by a small group of artist-jewelers in steering jewelry into the realm of art since the end of World War II. The momentum of this movement has been gaining up to the current generation of practitioners, who consider themselves primarily artists working in the medium of jewelry.

Artists working in traditional fine art mediums are reluctant to give jewelry the full status of "art." The process of emancipation that has occurred in painting and sculpture since the Renaissance is only now beginning to be extended to ceramics, glass, textiles, and jewelry. There are still many who resist this trend, affirming that jewelry, regardless of how it is conceived, is craft; craft, the making of functional articles, can never be art.

Much of modern art has resisted the idea of function; utility and aesthetic freedom are seen to be at odds. Many have suggested that in order to gain access into the pantheon of art, jewelry must eschew any function, as if attachment to the body were a form of enslavement or limitation. Art potters sometimes reacted to this expectation by creating pots that escaped all possibility of use; after all, industry provided plenty of well-designed vessels to hold things. Either way, ceramics has followed the nonutilitarian cues in its attempt to enter the realm of art.

As for furniture's claim to artistic status, one of its greatest practitioners, Gaetano Pesce, eloquently made the case:

> If an object is the bearer of a new creativity, a new language, of technical and material innovations, and moreover serves to satisfy a practical need, I do not see what prohibits its consideration as an example of fine art. . . . What counts is to provoke doubt, to create insecurity about established values.[3]

When applied to jewelry, the question of utility verges on the absurd. What is the function of jewelry anyway? Granted, jewelry has traditionally had functions—just as painting and sculpture once had—but these functions concern status, adornment, symbolism, ritual, and magic, and, to this day, commemoration of a sacred or sentimental event. Two of these functions—conveying the status of the wearer and serving as a form of portable wealth—have probably constrained the art jewelry movement more than any others. If the value of a work of jewelry rests on the merit of its artistry—the criterion of art jewelry—rather than on the value of precious materials, how can it convey the wealth and status of its owner?

Jewelry artists have an even steeper uphill battle winning artistic recognition from the public. Most people assume that art jewelry refers to work by well-known painters or sculptors, such as Louise Nevelson or Richard Pousette-Dart, or perhaps by famous designers of manufactured jewelry from a design house like Tiffany, such as Elsa Piretti or Paloma Picasso. Although these designers create notable jewelry, it is neither handmade nor one-of-a-kind; rather, it is generally designed on paper and produced in a workshop. Usually, multiple copies are produced.

It is symptomatic of the unclear position art jewelry holds in the American mind that it is necessary to define it here. Because the lines between various forms of jewelry are blurred, it might be easier to say what art jewelry is not. As noted above, it is *not* the latest creation of a famous designer or design house. It is *not* a fashion accessory or costume jewelry, which are commercial, mass-produced counterparts to current fashion trends without the depth or intent of art. Nor is it fine jewelry, which may be defined as conservative, usually traditional in design, utilizing precious metals and gemstones.

Furthermore, art jewelry is *not* craft jewelry, the handmade stuff of street fairs and craft shows, although it may oftentimes share certain characteristics, such as uniqueness and fine craftsmanship. Much craft jewelry is made in small production runs in art studios.

Jeweler John Iversen emphasized the differences among jewelry types in his comment, "Usually a good piece of 'fine jewelry' is a bad piece in any of the other categories, and a terrific piece of 'art jewelry' might look absolutely ridiculous if one views it as, for instance, fine or costume jewelry."[4] Making things even more confusing are jewelers like Iverson who make both production jewelry and unique art pieces.

What, then, is art jewelry? While it has many qualities, its most salient feature is its involvement with the issues of art: vision, intellect, and concept. In fact, it is more about art than about jewelry. According to Sarah Bodine, former editor of *Metalsmith*, one of art jewelry's most important journals (the other is *Ornament*), art jewelry is "unique pieces made by artists for expressive purposes." She continues, "If jewelry is not usually considered in the pantheon of fine art, it is because most people don't even know that this form exists. They just think of Tiffany."[5]

Oppi Untracht, Finnish metals critic and writer, offers this definition:

In contrast to most commercial jewelry, which is created by a designer and realized by a team of artisan-specialists, probably chiefly by mechanical means, today's art jewelers conceive the design and are fully capable of executing it—usually, but not always, by handwork methods. Their work possesses an immediacy and intimacy that only personal contact by the designer-maker with his or her materials can explain. Because this work incorporates such a high degree of conceptual and technological creativity, these jewelers are truly creative artists.[6]

These are works of art by artists that exist in the jewelry format, challenging both conventions and perceptions and always centered in the world of ideas. They are conceived, designed, and constructed primarily as art works, all else being secondary. Materials are subject to concept. Art jewelry, like all art, must seek new ground and must pose questions. "In the end," John Iversen explains, "it's how the person behind the work leads his/her life that gives the work its definition."[7]

We can easily assume the "life" Iversen is referring to is a life committed to art. All the works presented in this book are by people who consider themselves to be artists working in the realm of ideas, who for the most part create one-of-a-kind works entirely by themselves, and who are deeply concerned with the issues stated above. While none of these artists denigrates the craft component of their jewelry, most stress that the techniques and processes they master are not the sole purpose of what they do. Lisa Gralnick writes, "I have chosen to make jewelry, which is traditionally considered 'craft,' and I do enjoy the processes and techniques that allow me to execute my work without technical faults. But 'craft' is only a means to an end for me, as it is for many artists. My desire to push the limits of jewelry and expand on them, to comment on its traditions and associations, is more the concern of any artist."[8]

Who exactly is this art jeweler? Many are connected with metals programs in college and university art departments and are exposed to the intellectual environment of a university, which "develops aesthetically literate artists, who are well aware of the historical, philosophical, social, and psychological bases of artistic expression," explains Arline Fisch, ground-breaking jeweler and professor of art at San Diego State University. This education, she continues, teaches the artist to be both "articulate and self-critical." Another benefit, she notes, "is the pursuit of technical research and experimentation . . . a serious commitment to the investigation of materials and processes, both old and new."[9]

Jeweler Bruce Metcalf, one of the field's most prolific writers, gives us a profile of this new university-trained jeweler in his essay "On the Nature of Jewelry." This new type of jeweler:

> feels responsible to concepts and ideals alongside of the economic demands of making a living. Many jewelers insist that their production be completely divorced from the marketplace. To some, jewelry has become a pure expression of thought and feeling, and less connected to the traditional roles of ornament. Stripped of the familiar codes and functions, jewelry has become a modern art form.[10]

So where in the world of art do these art jewelers stand? Somewhere in a no-man's land between the fields of applied art and fine art, says Dutch art critic Gert Staal. Staal likens them to "borderland residents" living on the dividing line between two lands, "the indigenous population of an area enclosed between two territories . . . attired in the characteristics that both sides of that narrow line claim as their own." Rather than being a curse, Staal maintains that "in this duality lies their freedom . . . [they can] appropriate laws and customs of either side."[11]

The best art jewelry has gleaned from both of its homes a vast and rich inheritance. It melds the two fields into something unique and beautiful. Art jewelry transcends the basic work of goldsmithing and imbues it with an added dimension, the element of art.

Outside the shared terrain between jewelry and art, jewelers face an issue unique to them: wearability. It is generally assumed among the general public that all jewelry is to be worn; the idea of jewelry that cannot be worn or worn only with great difficulty is hard to accept. However, the conceptual nature of much contemporary jewelry demands free expression unrestricted by such corporeal concerns as: is it too big? Is it too heavy? Is it comfortable? Just as the creator of a chair may decide not to focus on ergonomics—even to make something that is not intended to be sat upon—a jeweler may choose to create a piece that is not really intended to be worn.

Jewelry artist Thomas Gentille writes:

> Jewelry as art form can fulfill the function of something which is worn, however it is an important distinction that this work need not be used. Often it is not displayed in the traditional "wearing" method, but shown using the same criteria as painting or sculpture. If worn, its usage requires a series of aesthetic judgments by the maker as well as the wearer. It is necessary that the work evokes some feeling beyond the configuration the piece takes, i.e., ring, armlet, pin or a form which is unique. Energies within the work, no matter how simple or

Charon Kransen. Hair pin. 1988. Wood, canvas, brass, wire, paint. Fabricated. 4 x 8 x ⅜". Photograph: Tom Haartsen

Valerie Mitchell. Stickpins. 1991. Hollow copper, silver, cement. Electroformed copper, patina. 8 x 7 x 1". Photograph: Mark Johann

14

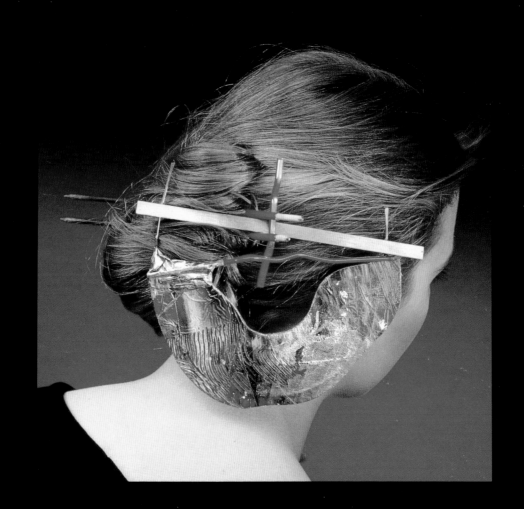
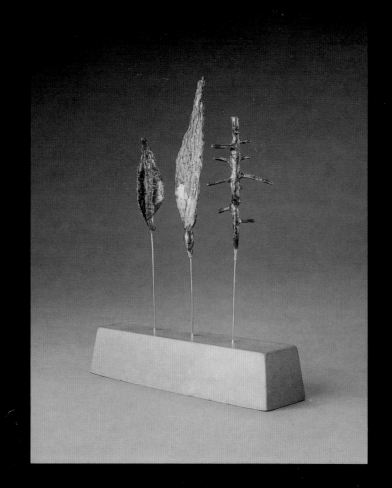

complex, quiet, or loud, are ones that must embody qualities beyond pure ornamentation.[12]

One might ask, if it can't be worn, is it really jewelry? The answer is, undeniably, yes. For much of this jewelry, the mere possibility of being worn is sufficient. An elaborate ring or neck piece may never touch someone's body but they always present the possibility of such contact. While this implicit wearability assures artistic freedom, it has limited the number of collectors in the field. Many jewelry wearers are unwilling to forsake the option of wearability, let alone the status of precious materials.

The issue of wearability is closely linked to that of scale, and scale continues to be a defining factor in jewelry and the one that attracts most artists to the medium, away from large-scale sculpture. Rather than perceiving small scale, or miniaturization, as a limitation and a constraint, most jewelers revel in the small-scale intricacies of their format. Several artists have managed to embody profoundly large concepts in a small-scale piece, even finding that the small scale aids the content of their work. There is also an attraction to the details and precision that can be exacted from a small piece; the same precision cannot be easily translated into a large-scale welded or carved sculpture. At the same time, jewelry has the unique advantage over all the other art forms in its direct contact with the human body, giving it an engaging intimacy.

A jeweler's preferred format is often dictated by concerns other than wearability. Pins and pendants are the most popular formats. A pin can sit on the chest like a painting or wall sculpture (Gentille and Warshaw) while a pendant becomes a three-dimensional sculpture. Hairpins and stick pins are valid formats that are less often explored (Rhein, Kransen, Mitchell).

Armlets, collars, neck rings, and torques are generally favored over traditional bracelets and necklaces, again for the artistic possibilities they allow. Though rings have few adherents, they, like Daniel Jocz, are enthusiastic about the medium. "I like the ring form because it makes a unified sculptural statement, allowing both formality and freedom. The constraint of the finger hole is great to play with sculpturally, sometimes adding a note of surprise or sometimes being celebrated, but most often its utilitarian purpose disappears in my work."[13] Earrings are generally considered too

Thomas Gentille. Pin. Bronze, translucent acrylic, 14- and 24-karat gold. Diam. 2⅞ x 9/16″

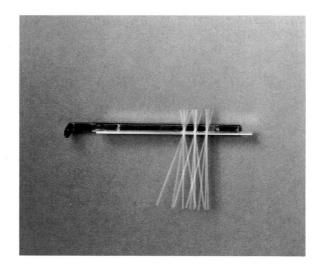

Alissa Warshaw. Brooch (at rest and in motion). 1990. Sterling silver, steel. Constructed. 2⅞ x 5 x ⅝″. Photographs: Bobby Hansson

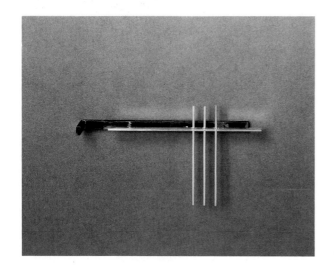

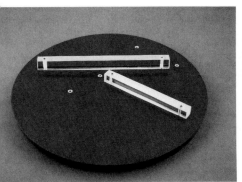

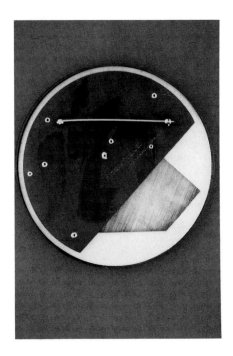

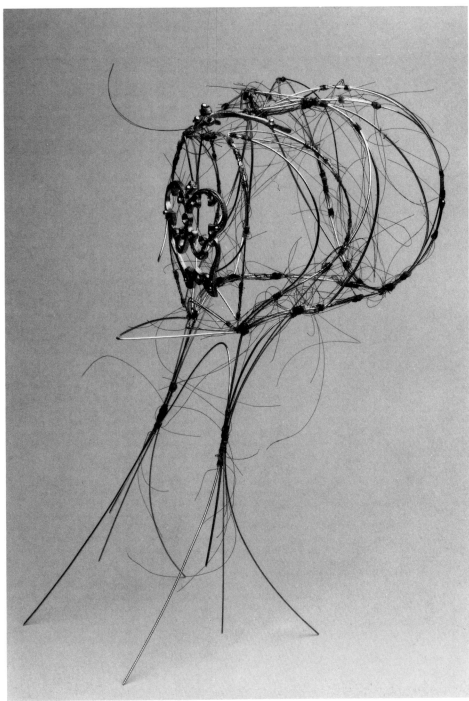

above left: Thomas Gentille. Hip pin (front and back). Bronze, acrylic, 14- and 24-karat gold. Diam. approx. 3½″. Photograph: Alan Fairley

above right: Eric Rhein. *Brian.* Hair comb. 1992. Steel, silver, gold wire, glue, nylon thread. Glued, constructed. Private collection. 9 x 4 x 4½″. Photograph: Jesse Frohman

constrained by functional requirements to allow the artist much freedom, Jill Slosberg-Ackerman being a prime exception. J. Fred Woell (see p. 39) "has given new life to such arcane forms as the medal and the trophy."[14]

While artist-jewelers draw freely from a wide array of contemporary art subjects and sources, a number wish to reconnect with jewelry's ancient ties to the symbolic and the mysterious. These are jewelry's heritage, its domain for millennia. The talismanic and magical properties of jewelry which bring luck, protect the wearer, and ward off negative forces have been embraced by Seattle jeweler Micki Lippi, with her totemic Spirit House pieces, and Marga Praxmarer, who combines her interest in

holistic medicine with jewelry to create amulets with "healing powers," bearing such names as *Ammunition of a Shaman*, *Earth Charm*, and *Incantations*.

Nor has the traditional concern with craftsmanship been abandoned. While modern art jewelry considers many issues besides craft, craftsmanship remains integral to its expression. The art jeweler takes on a commitment to make pieces as well as possible, down to the last detail. This workmanship is not used for its own sake but is placed at the service of a larger idea, adding credibility to concept.

Discussing the duality of concept and craftsmanship, Gentille has said, "No matter how great the concept, when the craftsmanship is not perfect the piece loses. You cannot see the concept for the poor craftsmanship. On the other hand, craftsmanship without concept is nothing."[15] Perfection for Gentille extends equally to the pin back as to its front.

Contemporary jewelry shares in common with both the fine and applied arts a

above left: Micki Lippe. *Spirit House Neck Piece.* 1992. Sterling silver, 22-karat gold, red jasper. Roll-printed, file-printed, fabricated. Pendant 3½ x ¾ x ¾". Private collection. Photograph: Richard Nicol

above right: Marga Praxmarer. *Witches Cauldron.* Necklace. 1991. Gold-plated sterling silver, shellac. Fabricated, assembled. Diam. 3½". Photograph: John Carlano

Linda MacNeil. Neck piece. 1983. Glass,
14-karat gold. Cast and acid-polished
glass. Private collection. Photograph: Susie
Cushner

multiplicity of styles and a profusion of materials. If the jeweler were to confine himself to the traditional resources of the jeweler's bench, his artistic range would be limited. Besides precious and nonprecious metals and all variety of stones, the art jeweler
borrows materials from the history of jewelry and from multiple cultures. The jeweler's materials include shells, clay and glass beads (Linda MacNeil), feathers, fabrics,
and, more recently, industrial materials like recycled parts from discarded machines
(Kris Benson uses parts from abandoned televisions). Foodstuffs like eggshells and
dried pasta have been used, as have plastics from resins to Formica-brand laminate,
and a wide variety of found objects, from beach pebbles to chewing-gum wrappers to
broken windshield glass to an old pair of nylons, placed on a gold background by
Marga Praxmarer to evoke the erotic.

   This new jewelry strives to be evaluated, like fine art, for its ideas, inventions,
intuitions, and content rather than for its preciousness or its conformity to tradition.

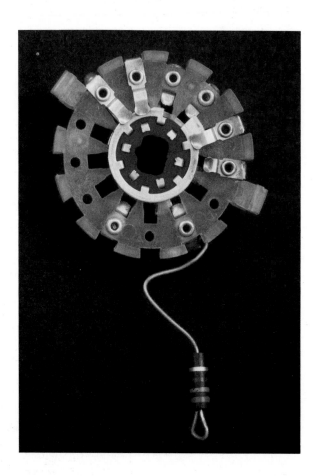

The reasons for rejecting precious, conventional jewelry materials are manifold: a delight in exploring new materials or the desire to question the nature of material possessions. Some jewelers go so far as to critique the entire fixation with jewelry as wealth, handed down from generation to generation like an insurance policy.

The work of German jeweler Otto Künzli beautifully illustrates this point. In his most famous bracelet, *Gold Makes Blind*, a golden ball is encased within a black rubber tube, its preciousness hidden from sight. The viewer and wearer are forced to take it on faith.

> This is perhaps a bauble for dangerous times; rubber does not tempt pickpockets. The hidden gold is the owner's secret to reveal or not. . . . Knowing the secret we enter a complicity with the owner, who in turn concluded a pact with the artist by blindly accepting the assertion that there is gold inside. And if it were instead fool's gold, what would the price of the object be? Is the artist's idea worth more or less than the current market price of the metal inside?[16]

Just as Künzli questions the value of gold, Myra Mimlitsch-Gray toys with our appreciation of diamonds by focusing on their abrasive character. Daniel Jocz cages gemstones, and Eleanor Moty explores the graphic potential of natural crystals like rutilated quartz rather than emphasizing their intrinsic value. Minimalist Eva Eisler continues her architectural explorations, for example, using diamonds as building blocks instead of status items.

above left: Kristen Benson. *Tel Collection Brooch.* 1991. Recycled television dial (plastic, silver). Constructed. 3 x 1 x ¼". Private collection. Photograph: Bobby Hansson

above right: Marga Praxmarer. *Nostalgia.* Brooch. 1989. Silver, niello, black nylon, gilded China paper. Fabricated and assembled. 3 x 3". Private collection. Photograph: John Carlano

opposite above: Otto Künzli. *Gold Makes Blind.* Arm piece. 1980. Rubber, gold. Diam. approx. 3". Photograph: Otto Künzli

opposite below: Otto Künzli. *Oh, Say!* Brooch. 1991. Gold. Approx. 3½ x 3½ x ¼". Private collection. Photograph: Otto Künzli

Daniel Jocz. *Caged Stone Series.* Ring. 1991. Two garnets, 14-karat gold, sterling silver. Soldered construction. 1¼ x 1 x ⅛". Collection the artist. Photograph: Dean Powell

opposite: Eva Eisler. Earrings. 1991. White gold, diamonds. Constructed. 3 x ⅓ x ¼". Collection Sandy Grotta, New Vernon, N.J. Photograph: George Erml

The challenge presented by the most mundane and everyday materials fascinates the contemporary jeweler. Take paper, for example, the antithesis of a costly material and the subject of intense artistic investigation. Dutch jeweler Nel Linssen has made spectacular necklaces of spiral overlapping paper elements. Tibbe Dunbar's paper brooches appear ethereal, almost ghostlike. Robert Ebendorf's paper beads and the Pijanowskis' papercord jewelry, seen later in these pages, demonstrate the artistic possibilities of this so-called worthless material.

Some jewelers are even returning to more precious materials, although, as Helen W. Drutt English, the single most important force behind art jewelry in America and owner of the pioneering Helen Drutt Gallery in Philadelphia, explained: "This is a time when Xerox copies, postcards and stamps can occupy the same position in a brooch as a ruby or a cameo."[17]

The multiplicity of styles—minimal, narrative, and organic—currently dominant in the fine and applied arts is reflected in art jewelry. Geometric formalism, Abstract Expressionism, and Minimalism had been the dominant styles since the exhibition "Modern Handmade Jewelry" at the Museum of Modern Art in 1946 (with brief detours into Pop art and narrative hippie jewelry in the 1960s). Pure form was what counted.

Today, Postmodernism—the mining of historical styles, literary references, and personal histories, the rediscovery of sensuousness and poetry, the questioning of the dogma of the International Style and the Bauhaus—has pointed jewelers in many new directions.

Nel Linssen. Necklace. 1991. Reinforced paper. Folded. Collection the artist. Photograph: Nel Linssen

Tibbie Dunbar. Brooch. 1990. Rice paper, steel wire. Constructed. 8 x 3″. Photograph: D. James Dee

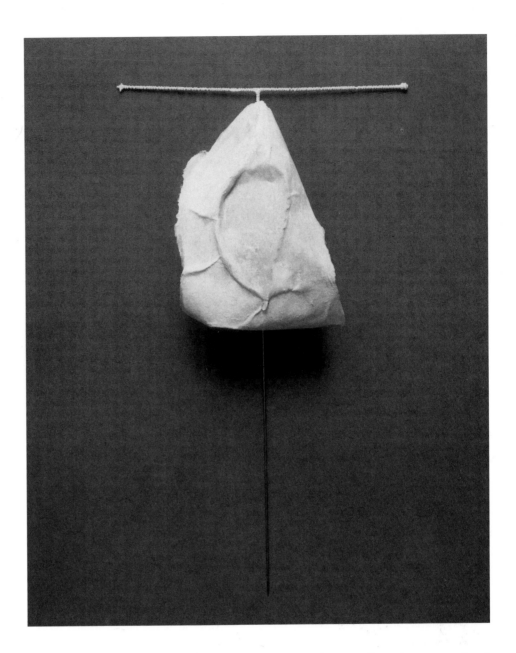

No longer are "the personal or emotional taboo," and no longer are "cool logic, calm calculation, straight lines and geometric shapes"[18] the only concern, as Yvonne G.J.M. Joris tells us in "Beauty Is a Story," held at the Het Kruithuis Museum in the Netherlands in 1991. Charon Kransen, one of the leading promoters of European jewelry in America, explains further, "Jewelry is giving shape to memories, stories from a diary."[19]

Narrative jewelry is jewelry that tells a story, whether based on fact, dream, or fantasy. It can be colorful and decorative or surreal and somber and sometimes contains text or language in its design. Jewelers like Joyce Scott, Kiff Slemmons, Laurie Hall, Beverly Penn, Kranitzky and Overstreet, Richard Mawdsley, Rebecca Batal, and Christina Smith are notable examples of jewelers who work in this mode. The new interest in the narrative also explains the shift in work seen in the pages on Sandra Sherman and Susan Hamlet.

Dutch critic Gert Staal pointed to this in his essay for the 1990 exhibition "American Dreams, American Extremes," also at the Het Kruithuis Museum. He noted:

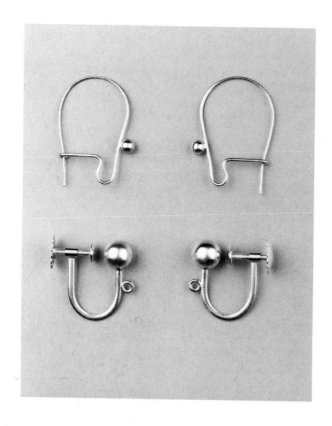

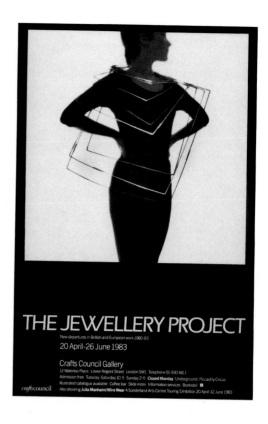

Narrative American pieces are more impudent—in size, use of material, esthetic expression—than those from the old world. . . . What distinguishes the American use of Xerox copies, postcards and stamps . . . is the world of fantasy that it opens up. . . . More tasteless, as the puritans might say, and because of their inscrutability, you note that after a while they become more intriguing.[20]

Which brings us to the extensive interaction and cross-fertilization between American and European jewelers. Despite their mutual influence, some generalizations can be made about their differences. European jewelry is by and large more occupied with problem solving and conceptual issues. It reveals a narrower focus and is more exclusive than the generally inclusive approach to materials and subjects found in American work. In the United States, one can find more personal narratives and emotional expression than in the cooler, more restrained European work. Humor is also more prevalent in American jewelry, an element found in Barbara Walter's punster rings or Joan Parcher's greatly enlarged earring jokes.

Another area of difference is the issue of wearability. "In Western Europe . . . the major influence in new jewelry is the idea that it must work with the body—a principle that is itself central to the original thinking of [Emmy] Van Leersum and [Gijs] Bakker,"[21] the parents of contemporary Dutch jewelry. Even the avant-garde selection of modern European work known as the Jewellery Project (1983) was "discreet and designed to work quietly with the wearer."[22]

American jewelers, on the other hand, often approach their work as art or sculpture and see the wearer as no more than an armature. This aspect prompted architectural historian James Ackerman to comment:

above left: Joan A. Parcher. *Kidney Ear Wire* and *Ear Screw Earrings.* 1990. Sterling silver. Fabricated. *Kidney Ear Wire Earrings* (above): 1¼ x 1¾ x ¼"; *Ear Screw Earrings* (below): 1⅜ x 1¼ x ⁷⁄₁₆". Photograph: Ric Murray

above right: The Jewellery Project: New Departures in British and European Work 1980 to 1983. Poster. Crafts Council Gallery, London, April 20 to June 26, 1983. Collection Malcolm and Sue Knapp, New York. Photograph: David Ward. Neck piece by Lam de Wolf. 1982. Painted fabric and wood

Gijs Bakker. *Dewdrop.* Necklace. 1982.
Laminated photograph. 19¼ x 20⅛″.
Collection Helen W. Drutt English,
Philadelphia. Photograph: Jos Fielmich,
Haarlem, the Netherlands

The artist-jeweler faces a wary or hostile public; most potential patrons or collectors—even those who might have daring taste in contemporary fine art—lack confidence to flout convention by making a statement in what they display on their bodies. The wearer of an object that does not conform to established custom becomes an exhibitor and must be personally committed in a way not demanded by objects of fine art or even by objects in other crafts traditions such as ceramics, all of which are impersonal in the sense of being detached from the body. A piece of jewelry normally completes its mission only when it is worn.[23]

The factor that unites all jewelry is its relationship to the body. Ackerman notes that even when the work is radical in form, it observes the typology of jewelry in Western culture to a surprising degree. He observed further:

> Some of the works are wearable in only a restricted sense, like those of Boris Bally, the wearer of which would be required to concentrate exclusively on avoiding damage to herself, her clothes and those around. Joan Parcher's ring and pendant of graphite—a particularly fragile material—transfer themselves to the user's fingers or clothes. . . . If these artists are, in a limited sense, reacting to the discouraging prospects of marketing thoroughly utilitarian work, they are more significantly addressing the major issues of the function of jewelry today: these are objects to ruminate upon.[24]

In closing, a few words about the works in the book. Aside from the fact that all are examples of art jewelry, as defined above, they share other criteria that merit their inclusion. All of the artists here have primarily worked and studied in the United States, and all continue to produce jewelry, by hand, to the present day. Each can boast an oeuvre marked by recognition and acclaim by peers in the field, having distinguished themselves through skill, vision, and the uniqueness of their explorations.

The designation "American," like any distinction based on nationalism, is a difficult one to define in this age of mass communication and quick travel. Several of the artists included in this book have studied and exhibited abroad, and many were even born outside of the United States. The extensive interaction and cross-fertilization between European, Asian, and American jewelers has resulted in many of the exciting traits that characterize American jewelry.

Though jewelry is still a relatively young art form, it has reached maturity in certain respects. Much of the terrain involving materials, techniques, and styles has been mapped out, with one or more areas gaining or receding in importance from time to time. The decade of the 1980s is marked not so much by exploration as by a refinement of the breakthroughs of the previous four decades. But while this jewelry speaks to history and tradition, it also addresses itself to contemporary conceptual and cultural issues. It is hard not to recognize the developments in this field when our intellects and passions are so artfully engaged by this new generation of jewelry artists. This broadened scope of jewelry is securing its irretrievable and, one hopes, irreversible place in contemporary art and culture.

A wish for jewelry's future was poetically expressed at Ornamenta I, 1989, in Pforzheim, Germany, a world's fair of art jewelry in a city dedicated to jewelry making. The catalogue reads:

> Let us create gardens rather than new boxes. Only then will jewelry be freed from old illusions of form, function, material and values. Free of handed-down dependencies there is suddenly room—with no ultimate definition for jewelry, an art like any other.[25]

Joan A. Parcher. *Graphite Pendulum-Pendant.* Neck piece. 1990. Soft graphite, oxidized sterling silver, stainless steel. Lathe-turned graphite, metal construction. Overall length 17½″, pendant 1⅞ x ⅞ x ⅞″. Collection the artist. Photograph: James Beards

NOTES:

1. Thomas Gentille, letter to author, August 5, 1993.
2. Toni Lesser Wolf, "The Intimate Art," *ARTnews* 20, no. 20 (November 1989): 124.
3. Gaetano Pesce, quoted in Peter T. Joseph, "The Critical Moment: Crossings, Alignments and Territories," paper presented at the First National Symposium on Criticism in the Craft Arts, New York University, New York, April 24–25, 1992.
4. John Iverson, interview with author, New York, March 1993.
5. Sarah Bodine, quoted in Wolf, "The Intimate Art," 123.
6. Oppi Untracht, Foreword, in Victoria & Albert Museum, *Masterworks of Contemporary American Jewelry: Sources and Concepts,* exhib. cat. (London: Victoria & Albert Museum, 1985).
7. Iverson, interview, March 1993.
8. Lisa Gralnick, letter to author, November 1989.
9. Arline M. Fisch, in Introduction, *American Jewelry Now,* exhib. cat. (New York: American Crafts Museum, 1985).
10. Bruce Metcalf, "On the Nature of Jewelry," in *Jewelry Australia Now,* ed. Bob Thompson (Crafts Council of Australia, 1989).
11. Gert Staal, "Dwellers in a No-Man's Land," in *London Amsterdam: New Art Objects from Britain and Holland,* exhib. cat. (London: Crafts Council Gallery; and Amsterdam: Galerie Ra and Galerie de Witte Voet, 1988), 9.
12. Thomas Gentille, correspondence to author based on his statement in Victoria & Albert Museum, Wally Gilbert-Thomas Gentille, exhib. cat. (London: Victoria & Albert Museum, 1987).
13. Daniel Jocz, "Artist Statement," correspondence to author, 1992.
14. Linda Norden, "Review, J. Fred Woell, C.K.D. Gallery, New York, N.Y.," *Metalsmith* 9, no. 3 (Summer 1989): 42.
15. Thomas Gentille, conversation with author on ideas formulated in late 1950s, 1990.
16. Ian Wardropper, *10 Goldsmiths,* exhib. cat. (Chicago: Rezac Gallery, 1988).
17. Helen W. Drutt English, Introduction, *Jewelry International,* exhib. cat. (New York: American Craft Museum, 1984).
18. Yvonne G.J.M. Joris, *Beauty Is a Story,* exhib. cat. ('s Hertogenbosch, the Netherlands: Het Kruithuis Museum, 1991), 8.
19. Charon Kransen, telefacsimile to author, December 14, 1993.
20. Gert Staal, *American Dreams, American Extremes,* exhib. cat. ('s Hertogenbosch, the Netherlands: Het Kruithuis Museum, 1990).
21. Peter Dormer and Ralph Turner, *The New Jewelry: Trends and Traditions* (New York: Thames and Hudson, 1985), 14.
22. Ibid.
23. James Ackerman, Introduction, *Personal Epiphanies: Jewelry's Gift,* exhib. cat. (Boston: Artists Foundation, 1990).
24. Ibid.
25. Veronika Schwarzinger, "Schmuck ist Kunst oder Schmuck oder Kunst ist Schmuck ist Schmuck ist Kunst oder Sc," in *International Exhibition of Contemporary Jewelry,* exhib. cat. (Pforzheim, Germany, 1989).

The Studio Jewelry Movement: 1940–80
Roots and Results

TONI GREENBAUM

The history of American jewelry as an art form is complex and fascinating. The first artists to form the nucleus of a new direction began working in the 1940s, and each is marked by certain aesthetic sensibilities. Since many of them continued producing into the following decades, there exists a great deal of overlap from the decades 1940 to 1980. The trends begun in one decade influenced and invigorated those that followed.

The cultural climate in the United States immediately following World War II was ripe for the craft revival that ensued. This renaissance occurred in all mediums: clay, glass, fiber, wood, and metal. There were many reasons for this, but by far the most important were the desire to explore an entirely new artistic expression and a general trend toward a simpler and less stressful way of life after the trauma of World War II. It was also partly a reaction against the somewhat sterile and antihuman machine aesthetic that defined the product design of the late 1920s and 1930s.

Before the war, several factors contributed to setting the stage for the craft revival. Political turmoil in Europe during the 1930s brought many important artists and craftspeople to the safety and freedom of the United States. Schools such as Black Mountain College in Asheville, North Carolina, and the School (later Institute) of Design in Chicago (often referred to as the New Bauhaus) reaped the benefits of these extraordinary refugees, including Josef and Anni Albers at Black Mountain College and László Moholy-Nagy at the School of Design.

In 1940, the Handcraft Cooperative League of America, under the leadership of Aileen Osborn Webb, opened America House in New York City, the first retail outlet devoted to American contemporary crafts. In 1942, the American Craftsmen's Cooperative Council was founded, consolidating two independent organizations: the Handcraft Cooperative League of America and the American Handcraft Council. The ACCC's mandate was to serve as a vehicle for furthering craft education and promoting retail sales of handmade objects. That same year, the organization began publishing *Craft Horizons* (now called *American Craft*). To further the ACCC's educational

opposite: Merry Renk. Wedding crown. 1968. 14-karat gold sheet, wire, cultured pearls. 2¾ x 6¾" (diam). Collection American Craft Museum, New York. Gift of S. C. Johnson, Inc. From the Johnson Collection of Contemporary Crafts. Photograph: M. Lee Fatheree, courtesy American Craft Museum, from the exhibition "Jewelry from the Permanent Collection," 1978

goals, the American Craftsmen's Educational Council, Inc., was inaugurated in 1943. The ACEC provided library facilities and presented exhibitions, in addition to supporting training programs in the crafts for returning veterans. (After several more modifications and name changes, since 1979 the combined ACCC and ACEC has been called the American Craft Council.)

At least three decades prior to the end of the war, the precedent had been set for the education of metalsmiths, since the making of jewelry had been offered in normal schools as part of the teacher-training curriculum and in public school manual arts programs. For men returning from the military, metalsmithing was deemed, and proved to be, excellent occupational therapy. Programs teaching metalsmithing and jewelry making began to be offered at various colleges, such as Cranbrook Academy of Art in Michigan, the University of Kansas, and Indiana University. These craft courses could be easily justified as they fulfilled the socially commendable purpose of training war veterans. Some public institutions undertook similar programs, such as the War Veterans' Art Center at the Museum of Modern Art in New York.

At the same time, to counteract the emphasis on occupational therapy, as well as to produce craft objects of real and outstanding quality, the Rehabilitation Training Program at Dartmouth College, sponsored by the American Craftsmen's Educational Council, was renamed the School for American Craftsmen in 1944. The focus had been altered to suit the needs of the professional maker. Within a year the school became part of the Fine and Hand Arts Division at Alfred University in Alfred, New York. A practical approach to metalsmithing was emphasized, and hollowware was given emphasis over jewelry. Students were ostensibly trained to make a living at their craft.

Among the school's noteworthy metals students were Fred Fenster, Arline Fisch, John Paul Miller, Ronald Hayes Pearson, Svetozar and Ruth Radakovich, and Olaf Skoogfors. Pearson credits jeweler Philip Morton with being his initial mentor at the School for American Craftsmen. Probably due to Morton's emphasis on the importance of aesthetics rather than practicality, he was replaced in 1948 by John Prip.[1] Prip had been trained in Denmark and adapted the functional Scandinavian approach to the production of American hollowware and, to a lesser extent, jewelry,

Ruth Penington. *Ermine Tails Neck Piece.*
1971. Sterling silver, ermine tails. 12 x 12″.
Collection Anne G. Hauberg, Seattle.
Photograph: Brian Russell, courtesy The
National Ornamental Metal Museum,
Memphis, Tenn.

although his propensity for new ideas ultimately led him to become an innovator in his own right. The school again relocated in 1950, this time to become part of the Rochester Institute of Technology, Rochester, New York. RIT's approach did not substantially change when another Dane, Hans Christiansen, took the helm of the RIT metals department in 1954. Christiansen, then head of the model department at Georg Jensen in Copenhagen, was a strict proponent of the Danish Modern style, which exalted in structure and unadorned surfaces. The philosophy at the school was not to alter until Albert Paley joined the faculty in 1969.

Hand in hand with the postwar education of young jewelers, academic interest in jewelry as an art form grew. Concurrent with the development of the School for American Craftsmen were five important Silversmithing Workshop Conferences, one held each summer from 1947 through 1951, begun by Margret Craver and sponsored by Handy and Harman Metal Refiners, New York. The School for American Craftsmen hosted two of the workshops. Among the important jewelers attending the conferences were Alma Eikerman, John Paul Miller, Robert A. Von Neumann, Earl Pardon, and Ruth Penington.

Jewelry also became the subject of major exhibitions. The Museum of Modern Art in New York City mounted "Modern Jewelry Design" as early as 1946. This exhibition emphasized innovation over technical perfection, displaying designs of great spirit and vitality that incorporated unusual materials, including safety pins, and a variety of hardware. The works exhibited revealed a strong reaction against the prevalent conventional design of much commercial, costume, and traditional jewelry. The Museum of Modern Art curators primarily chose jewelry created by craftspeople but also included examples made by painters and sculptors, among them Richard Poussette-Dart, Alexander Calder, and Jacques Lipschitz. The "fine" artists were thought to lend credibility to the jewelers, such as Paul Lobel, Margaret de Patta, and Adda Husted-Anderson.

Nothing like this exhibition had been seen before; most of the concepts were

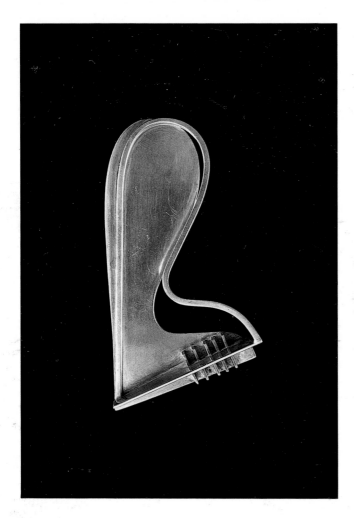

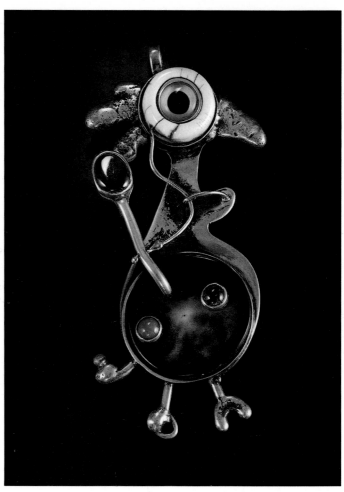

totally new. For example, Anni Albers, also a remarkable weaver, and Alex Reed (a student of hers at Black Mountain College) were represented by a necklace made from a sink drain and paper clips. The exhibition traveled to, among other places, the Art Museum at Rhode Island School of Design, Providence. Following the Museum of Modern Art's lead, the Walker Art Center in Minneapolis organized "Jewelry for Under $50" in 1948, 1955, and 1959. These were traveling exhibitions and were thus responsible for introducing people across the country to the new handmade jewelry.

Although the ACCC was originally comprised of regional affiliates, independent local organizations (an outgrowth of the craft "guilds" dating back to the Arts and Crafts movement of the early twentieth century), offering support systems to craftspeople, began to form. One such organization, the Metal Arts Guild (MAG), founded in northern California in 1951, included Milton Cavagnaro, Peter Macchiarini, Margaret de Patta, Merry Renk, Florence Resnikoff, and Irena Brynner (who moved to New York in 1956).

Among the most original and influential pioneering jewelers in New York City were Sam Kramer, Paul Lobel, Art Smith, and Ed Wiener; Earl Pardon in Saratoga Springs, New York; and Margaret de Patta and Bob Winston in northern California. The leitmotiv that bound all of these studio jewelers together was the desire to apply the then current tenets of modernism, such as biomorphism, primitivism, and constructivism to jewelry.

In 1944, Paul Lobel was one of the first jewelers to open a studio/shop in

above left: Paul Lobel. *Piano.* Brooch. c. 1940s. Sterling silver. Fabricated. Collection Mark Isaacson and Mark McDonald. Photograph: Courtesy Fifty/50, New York

above right: Sam Kramer. *Roc Pendant.* 1967. Sterling silver, 14-karat gold, ivory, horn, coral, taxidermy eye, tourmaline, garnet. Cast, constructed, fused. 4¾ x 2¼ x ¾". Collection American Craft Museum, New York. Museum purchase, 1967. Donated to The American Craft Museum by The American Craft Council, 1990. Photograph: Eva Heyd

34

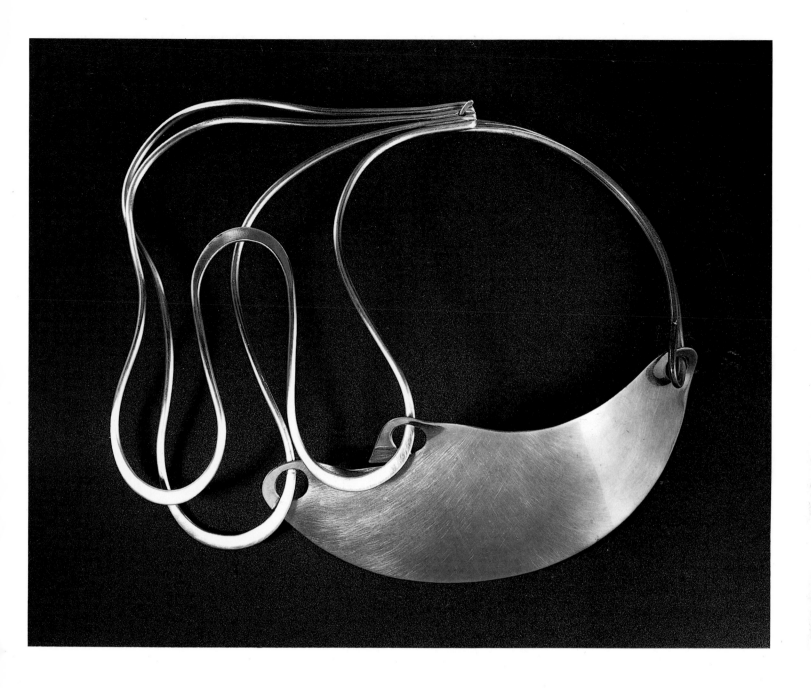

Art Smith. Neck piece. 1948. Brass. Forged. 7¾ x 6 x 1⅝". Collection American Craft Museum, New York. Museum purchase, 1967. Donated to The American Craft Museum by The American Craft Council, 1990. Photograph: Eva Heyd

Greenwich Village. His enterprise became the prototype for those of Art Smith and Ed Wiener (who had another store on West Fifty-third Street). Lobel's style was simpler than that of his peers. He employed few or no stones and relied solely on the sculptural potential of flat metal sheet and wire to express his design idiom.

Sam Kramer, his antithesis, who also operated a studio/shop, produced surreal creations related to themes of the unconscious, automatic writing, and dream imagery. He experimented with fusing molten bits of silver, often with haphazardly scattered semiprecious stones, which were chosen for their color and texture rather than their intrinsic value. Kramer also used found objects, such as shells, bits of meteorites, and glass taxidermy eyes.

Art Smith also drew inspiration from Surrealism. He adapted biomorphic forms, using a language similar to that in the painting and sculpture of Joan Miró, to create sculptural mobilelike jewelry for the human body. Smith viewed the body as an armature for the work, an extraordinary and unprecedented concept for his day.

35

Ed Wiener took a more eclectic approach. Exploring many different aesthetic trends, he produced a body of work that expressed the mid-twentieth-century jewelers' desire to align themselves with modern art movements. His work sometimes reflected the Cubism of Alexander Archipenko and occasionally the childlike whimsy of Paul Klee. Wiener has said that wearing a piece of modernist jewelry was akin to sporting a badge that proclaimed one's affinity with modern art.[2]

Along with interpreting modern art movements, another dominant trend of the late 1940s was primitivism. As early as the late 1930s, Alexander Calder and Harry Bertoia began employing a direct, empirical treatment of metal wire and sheet. Earl Pardon's jewelry from the 1940s and early 1950s exemplifies this treatment of silver. The jewelry was forged and the individual elements were connected, allowing hammer marks, rivets, and hinges to become an integral part of the overall design. In this technical sense, Pardon's jewelry is reminiscent of the turn-of-the-century Arts and Crafts movement, and in form, it recalls African and Oceanic sculpture. He also created fantastic creatures at this time, which, like Wiener's, recalled the work of Klee.

Concurrently in San Francisco, Bob Winston was exploring metal-casting techniques, while Margaret de Patta transposed the Constructivist principles of émigré artist László Moholy-Nagy into jewelry. In 1941, de Patta studied with Moholy-Nagy at the School of Design in Chicago. She followed his admonitions when he told her to consider the possibility of designing pieces as if they were three-dimensional structures made up of planes that intersected at oblique angles with stones that seemed to float freely in space.[3] De Patta mounted stones, eccentrically cut to her specifications by lapidary Francis Speresin, in "invisible" settings and experimented with optical illusions created by light refractions passing through the stones. Between de Patta and Speresin, they developed extraordinary uses of light refraction and asymmetrical faceting and gave life and vitality to some semiprecious stones, such as rutilated quartz, never before exposed in their structures. This treatment of stones was entirely new, and these works are simultaneously scientific and poetic. De Patta was an immensely influential, innovative, and populist jeweler. She not only created dynamic, one-of-a-kind designs but also devised a method of producing limited editions of select pieces. It was her hope to give a wide spectrum of people the opportunity to purchase her jewelry, and she encouraged other jewelers to seek business venues as well.[4] Several jewelers managed to maintain a great deal of design integrity within the scheme of production. Betty Cooke (Baltimore), Ed Levin (Vermont and later Cambridge, New York), and Ronald Hayes Pearson (Deer Isle, Maine) are but three who each managed to develop a range of designs appropriate to limited production methods, which were welcome additions to many shops and craft outlets.

In the 1950s several shops and galleries dedicated to the display and sale of fine crafts were inaugurated. One of the most influential was Shop One, opened in Rochester, New York, in 1952 by John Prip, Ronald Hayes Pearson, ceramist Frans Wildenhain, and woodworker Tage Frid. In 1956 the Museum of Contemporary Crafts, an affiliate of what was then called the American Crafts Council, was founded, a major event in the world of fine crafts. Like the ACC, it came about thanks to the vision of Aileen O. Webb. The Museum of Contemporary Crafts (renamed in 1979 the American Craft Museum) was the first museum in the United States dedicated exclusively to furthering contemporary American crafts. The 1960s gave rise to com-

J. Fred Woell. *The Good Guys.* Pendant. 1966. Walnut, steel, copper, plastic, silver, gold leaf. Constructed. Diam. 4 x ½″. Collection American Craft Museum, New York. Gift of The Johnson Wax Company, from OBJECTS: USA, 1977. Donated to The American Craft Museum by The American Craft Council, 1990. Photograph: Eva Heyd

opposite: Abraham [Christian Schmidt]. *Medal of Honor.* 1964. Metal, semiprecious stones, cameo. Assembled. Length 9¼″. Collection Minnesota Museum of Art, Saint Paul. Acquisition Fund Purchase

petitions and craft fairs, many of which continue today, intended to promote the crafts in all mediums. Handwrought jewelry was consistently one of the most sought-after items.

The cultural and political turbulence of the 1960s spawned a group of staunch individualists representative of the counterculture, which was fighting to make itself noticed. These artists, who considered themselves outsiders and outcasts, championed what has come to be known as Pop and Funk. Along with the Dadaists and Surrealists, although quite differently, they created some of the most idiosyncratic jewelry that this century had yet produced. Furthermore, it was work that was socially relevant and somewhat antiprecious, so as jewelry it risked losing a traditional audience.[5]

The first piece of Pop jewelry documented was *Medal of Honor*, made by Christian Schmidt (Minneapolis) in 1964. Schmidt combined assorted semiprecious gemstones, bits of wire, and found objects, such as a small cameo and a tin toy sheriff's badge, into a neck piece. Intended as a satirical statement about the jurying process, it was made specifically for an exhibition at the Saint Paul Art Center held that same year and submitted under the pseudonym "Abraham." Ironically, the piece was enthusiastically accepted.

J. Fred Woell (Boston and later Deer Isle, Maine) soon followed suit with *The Good Guys* in 1966. This pendant, four inches in diameter and composed of gold-painted wood, staples, and plastic buttons showing images of the Red Cross and Superman, Little Orphan Annie, and Dick Tracy, elevates comic strip characters to the status of icons. Emphasizing content, Woell rejected the precious materials from which jewelry had been traditionally made, although he endowed the pendant with a Byzantine form, thereby linking it with the continuum of Western jewelry design.

Funk jewelry, like the painting and sculpture movement of the same name that originated in California, was similar in concept to Pop but was often additionally imbued with banal or blatant sexual imagery. This was jewelry intended to shock, and it did. Ken Cory (Seattle; often collaborating with Les LePere as the "Pencil Brothers") was perhaps the best of the Funk jewelers. He employed organic, sensual forms of cast plastic or leather with copper, stones, often narrative enamelwork, and found objects.

Another jeweler who used found objects, albeit in an almost tribal manner, was Ramona Solberg, who now also lives in Seattle and has taught at the University of Washington. Solberg combined primitive, folk, and contemporary detritus with wrought and electroformed metal elements to create neck pieces replete with nostalgia and symbolism.

The movement toward an assertive individualism made itself felt even in the academic world. Albert Paley, who joined the faculty of RIT in 1969, fabricated dramatic, sculptural jewelry to be worn by self-assured, liberated women. Rejecting the school's traditional emphasis on hollowware, he took advantage of the purely artistic potential that jewelry afforded. Paley believed ornamentation and structure should be integrated. He advocated the undulant forms of Art Nouveau and the emotional fervor of Abstract Expressionism, which he eclectically combined and reinterpreted in large-scale neck pieces and brooches.

The revival of historical techniques was another important trend of the 1960s. Margret Craver (Boston) reinvented the obscure and lost late Renaissance technique of *en résille* enameling. In this process, enamel is not fused to a single metal backing, as is usually the case, but rather individual small enameled metal elements float on a crystal quartz or glass surface. Craver set the enamel into a shardlike unit, which she then mounted in a gold brooch, pendant, or hair ornament.

John Paul Miller (Cleveland) rediscovered the ancient Etruscan art of granulation, which had been lost for nearly two thousand years. This is a process whereby tiny gold balls are adhered to a gold background through a molecular exchange process, creating a "carpet" of gold granules on the work's surface. Miller combined his granulation technique with plique-à-jour and cloisonné enameling on pieces that are unique stylizations of natural forms such as sea urchins and insects.

Phillip Fike (Detroit) intensively studied ancient forms such as the fibula, a clasp resembling a safety pin used by the Greeks, Etruscans, and Romans, and the manner in which various parts of pieces of jewelry are connected, devising unique ways of incorporating these connections into his overall designs. This was not unlike, incidentally, the devotion to process exhibited by the turn-of-the-century Arts and Crafts movement jewelers, as well as Earl Pardon, discussed earlier.

The jewelry of Alma Eikerman (Bloomington, Indiana) is representative of yet another important midcentury trend: the exploration of open and continuous forms in space and the relationship of solids and voids and how they mutually define one another.[6] Eikerman's work was forged, while the spiritually similar undulating forms of Ronald Hayes Pearson and Svetozar and Ruth Radakovich (Encinatas, California) were mostly cast. The Radakoviches often combined several techniques, such as casting and forging, within one piece, creating a tense relationship of forms. Their work

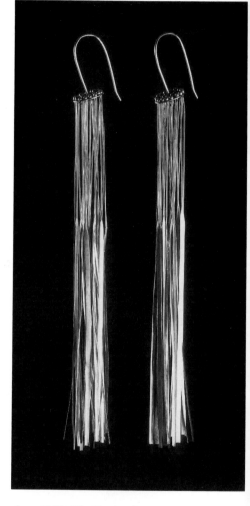

above: Phillip Fike. Earrings. 1968. 14-karat white and yellow gold. Forged. 3¾ x ½″. Collection American Craft Museum, New York. Gift of The Johnson Wax Company, from OBJECTS: USA, 1977. Donated to The American Craft Museum by The American Craft Council, 1990. Photograph: Eva Heyd

opposite: John Paul Miller. *Dung Beetle.* Pendant/Brooch. 1989. 18-karat and pure gold. Fabricated, granulated, enameled. 2¾ x 1¼ x ⅝″. Private collection. Photograph: John Paul Miller

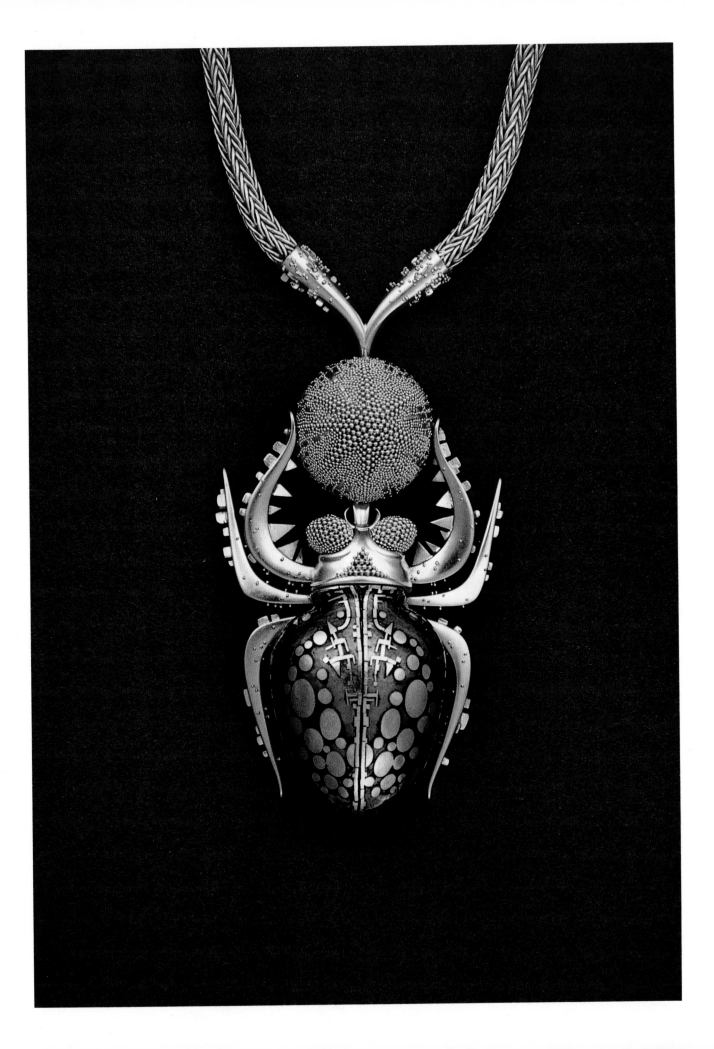

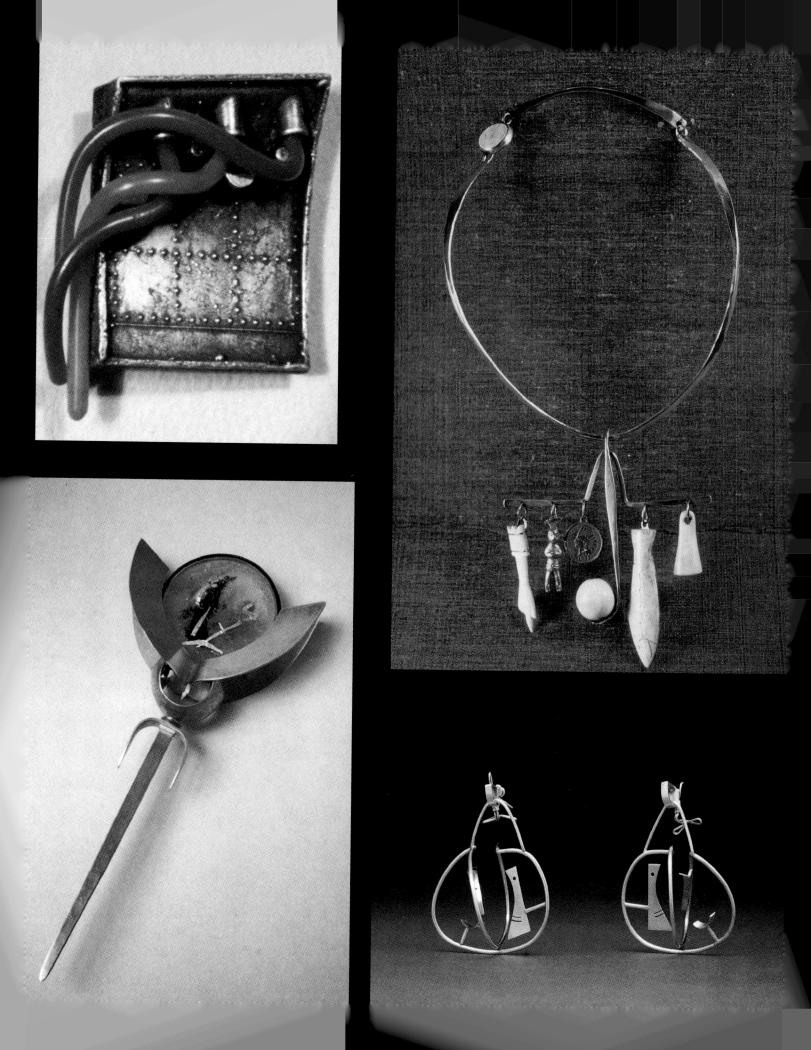

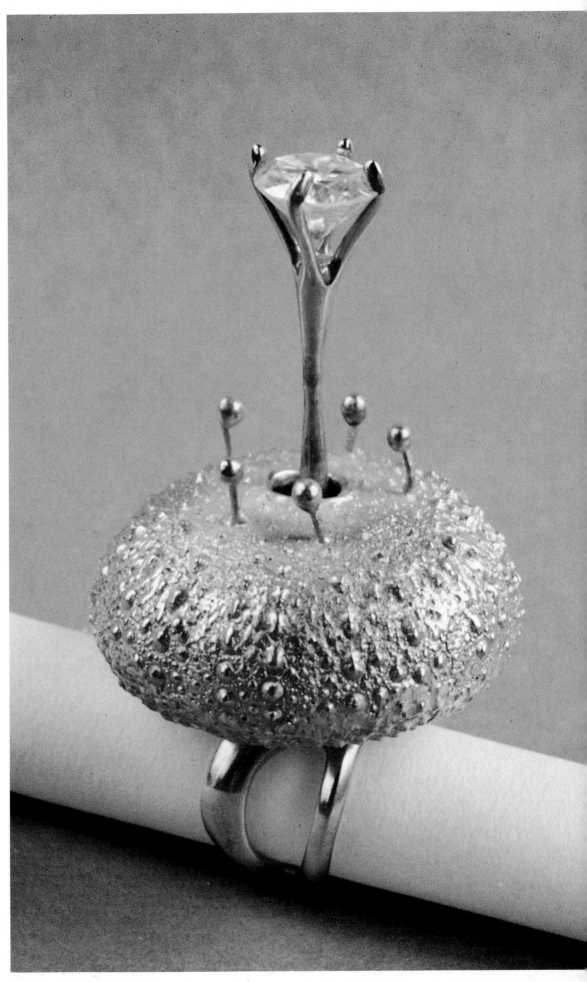

opposite above left: Ken Cory. Pin. 1968. Cast silver and Plexiglas. 1³/₄ x 2¹/₂ x ¹/₂″. Photograph: Courtesy American Craft Museum, from the exhibition "Objects Are . . .?," 1968

opposite above right: Ramona Solberg. *Shaman's Necklace.* 1968. Silver, Alaskan ivory, found objects. Fabricated. Length 16¹/₄″. Photograph: Ferdinand Boesch, courtesy American Craft Museum, from the exhibition "Objects USA," 1969

opposite below left: Margret Craver. Hair ornament. 1959. Yellow gold, en resille enamel. 5³/₄ x 2¹/₂″. Collection American Craft Museum, New York. Museum purchase, 1959. Donated to The American Craft Museum by The American Craft Council, 1990. Photograph: Bobby Hansson

opposite below right: Alma Eikerman. *Sculptural Earrings.* 1963. Sterling silver. Constructed. 3¹/₄ x 2¹/₂ x 2¹/₂″. Private collection

right: Ruth Radakovich. *Cocktail Ring.* 1969. 14-karat gold, titanium rutile. 2³/₄ x 1³/₄″. Collection American Craft Museum, New York. Gift of The Johnson Wax Company, from OBJECTS: USA, 1977. Donated to The American Craft Museum by The American Craft Council, 1990. Photograph: Bobby Hansson

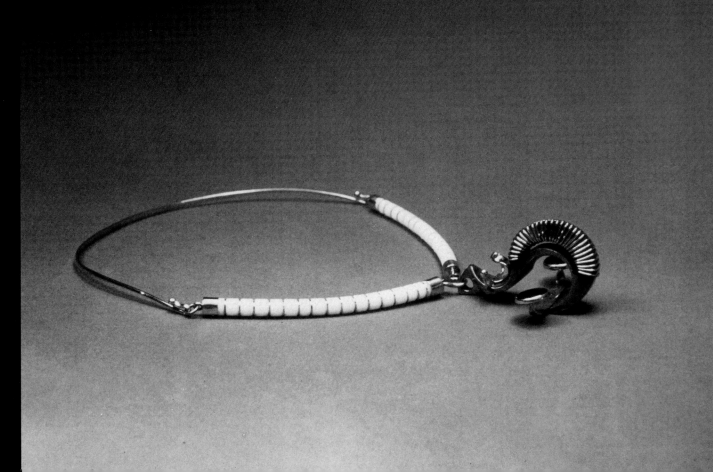

from the 1960s and early 1970s investigates the connection between tenuous line juxtaposed with more solid volumes. Fred Fenster (Wisconsin) also utilized a combination of forging, fabrication, and casting techniques. He altered simple forms through cutting, twisting, and compression to create a sense of movement and transition.[7]

While many jewelers explored three-dimensional forms in space, Olaf Skoogfors (Philadelphia) focused in part on the investigation of surface effects and textures. His work was strongly affected by Abstract Expressionism, whose influence began to be seen anew in jewelry in the 1970s. He achieved his surfaces by applying textures to wax forms and then casting them, resulting in brooches that may be viewed as grainy bas reliefs. Atypically, instead of treating stones and pearls as central elements, he used them as exclamation points.[8] Heikki Seppa (Saint Louis) also highlighted surface texture, through his use of reticulation. However, his greatest innovation was defining forms in space with his invention of the shell-casting technique.

Skoogfors was very interested in European work and traveled abroad to study and visit the studios of major European metalsmiths. Two of these trips were made with fellow Philadelphia jeweler Stanley Lechtzin in 1965. Skoogfors was represented in the "Dürer 500th Anniversary" exhibition in Nuremburg in 1970. The enthusiasm he evinced—in common with the World Craft Council, Helen Drutt, Stanley

Lechtzin, Robert Ebendorf, and Arline Fisch, among others—for European work was one of the contributing factors to the intensive German influence on American jewelry that was to make itself strongly felt in the mid-1970s.

Lechtzin has explored and adapted modern industrial technology to create large-scale yet lightweight jewelry, enlisting the process of electroforming metal in combination with mineral crystals and plastics. Using the tools and techniques traditionally reserved for industry he has achieved the effect of organic growth, and through electroforming he pioneered the incorporation of materials that had previously not been possible to mount.

In November 1968 in Chicago, Philip Morton held a meeting with Robert Ebendorf, Phillip Fike, Hero Kielman, Brent Kington, Stanley Lechtzin, Kurt Matzdorf, Ronald Hayes Pearson, and Olaf Skoogfors to organize an American guild of contemporary jewelers and metalsmiths. It was the genesis of the Society of North American Goldsmiths (SNAG). Many of the founding members were the vanguard of the contemporary movement. SNAG has probably done more to promote jewelry as an art form during the course of its twenty-five-year history than any other organization in the United States through its offering of numerous educational opportunities to metalsmiths and the championing of quality works. Its premier magazine *Metalsmith* (formerly *Goldsmith's Journal*) is currently the most important and informative vehicle for contemporary American jewelry.

The first International Conference of Metalsmiths, sponsored by the Society of North American Goldsmiths, was held in Saint Paul, Minnesota, in March 1970. It offered an exhibition—the first of many—entitled "Goldsmith '70." The show, cosponsored by the Minnesota Museum of Art, Saint Paul, and juried by Stanley Lechtzin and John Prip, featured 129 works by American and Canadian metalsmiths, representing all the major trends discussed. The exhibition was shown at the Museum of Contemporary Crafts, New York, from June to September 1970.

Among the jewelers included in "Goldsmith '70" was Miye Mitsukata (Boston). She was a jeweler who used both precious and semiprecious stones and found objects, such as ancient coins and beads, in such a way that they carried equal visual weight with her multitextured and varicolored gold. This focus has a different effect from Skoogfors's use of stones as punctuation marks, although she was influenced by the work of both Skoogfors and Lechtzin. She exhibited with them at the Odakyu Department Store in Tokyo in 1968. Mitsukata studied with two other luminaries in the jewelry field, first with William Harper, with whom she took enameling classes at Penland School of Crafts in Penland, North Carolina, and at Florida State University in Tallahassee, and then with Arline Fisch, at Boston University. It was Arline Fisch who inspired Mitsukata to crochet metal wire into torquelike necklaces, which she combined with antique Chinese textiles to form "collages" of metal and fiber.

Arline Fisch (San Diego) is probably best known for her pioneering adaptation of textile techniques like weaving, knitting, and crocheting to metal. In the mid-1960s, relatively early in her career, she used silver, sometimes combined with fiber, to create large, flexible collars and necklaces as well as full-length body ornaments that extended from the neck to the floor. In 1969 she eliminated the fiber elements and began to weave and knit completely in metal, sometimes adding feathers or mosaics or semiprecious stones to produce fascinating textural juxtapositions.

opposite above: Miye Matsukata. Pin/Necklace. 18-karat gold, opals. Shakudo. 8½ x 5″. Photograph: Bobby Hansson, courtesy American Craft Museum, from the exhibition "The Goldsmiths," 1974

opposite: Arline Fisch. Collar. 1975. Fine silver wire, sterling silver, 18-karat gold. Knitted, woven, fabricated. 7½ x 16 x 5″. Collection the artist. Photograph: Courtesy American Craft Museum, from the exhibition "Three Metalsmiths II: Fisch/Kington/Skoogfors," 1976

46

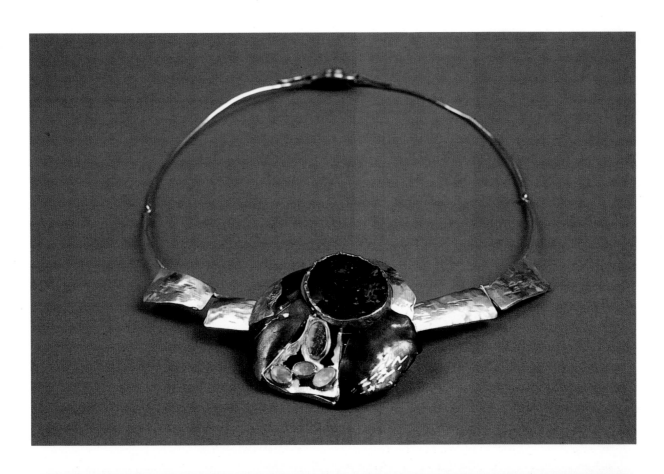

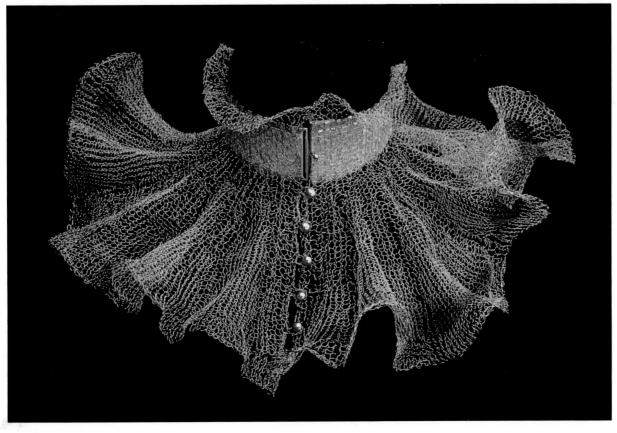

Mary Lee Hu (Seattle) began her experiments with fabric constructions in metal in the late 1960s. Her style is more controlled and her metal "fabrics" more structured and less flexible than Fisch's. Hu's woven patterns are considerably more complex and detailed. There is an Oriental and meditative quality to the way the surface proceeds from one end to the other, creating an equivalent in metal for the processes of weaving, plaiting, and so on.

Two other jewelers who, in the 1970s, turned to the East for technical and artistic inspiration were Gene Pijanowski and Hiroko Sato Pijanowski (Ann Arbor, Michigan). They studied traditional Japanese techniques of combining varicolored metals, for example, *mokume-gane* (wood-grained metal), and alloys, such as *shakudo* (gold and silver) and *shibuichi* (silver and copper), and adapted them to Western jewelry forms. Although not the first to do so, they often designed an "environment" for their jewelry, such as a stand or background drawing for the jewelry to be placed on when it was not being worn, as well as suites of several pieces, mostly brooches, to be worn and displayed in a series.

This concept of site-specific placement of jewelry was one that was brought to America via German artist/jeweler Claus Bury. Bury came to the United States in 1973 and spoke in the metals programs at several universities. Bury's visit proved to be a watershed; his inventive use of bonded acrylic and metal in mechanistic "landscapes," along with his application of jewelry as one element in a sculpture or diagram, altered the course of American jewelry history, away from the ornamental toward the conceptual. Although "concept" in jewelry was hitherto virtually unknown, there were a few American jewelers already experimenting in this direction. Robert Ebendorf, who taught in the metals department at the State University of New York at New Paltz and has been a well-known jeweler since the 1960s, was deeply influenced by Bury's treatment of jewelry as a pure art form and, in his turn, contributed greatly to the acceptance of jewelry as something more than simple adornment. With a personal visual language expressed through collages and assemblages made from elements as diverse as diamonds, paper, photographs, plastic, and found objects, Ebendorf has successfully investigated the concept of contradiction, thereby stretching the boundaries that had hitherto defined jewelry.

above left: Mary Lee Hu. *Neck Piece #9.* 1973. Fine and sterling silver, 24-karat gold, gold-filled brass, pearls. Wrapped, looped, woven. 12½ x 9½ x 7″. Collection the artist. Photograph: Mary Lee Hu

above right: Robert W. Ebendorf. *Mother and Child.* Brooch. 1971. Copper, sterling silver, paper, Plexiglas, found objects. Diam. 4¾″. Collection the artist. Photograph: T. Nakamura

opposite: Claus Bury. Brooch. 1977. Silver, gold, and copper alloys. 2 x 1¾″. Collection Helen W. Drutt English, Philadelphia. Photograph: Bobby Hansson, Courtesy SNAG Archives

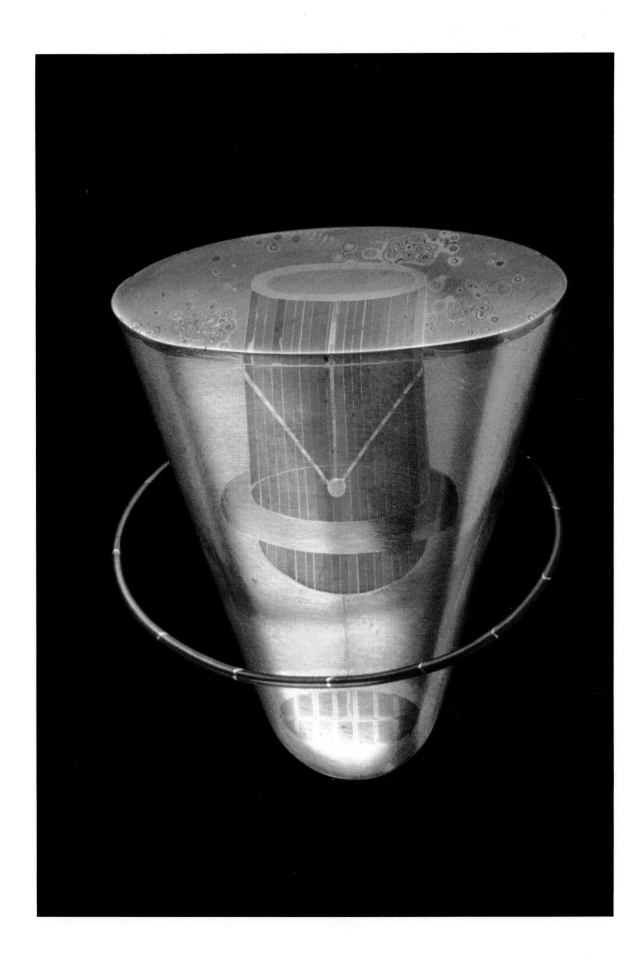

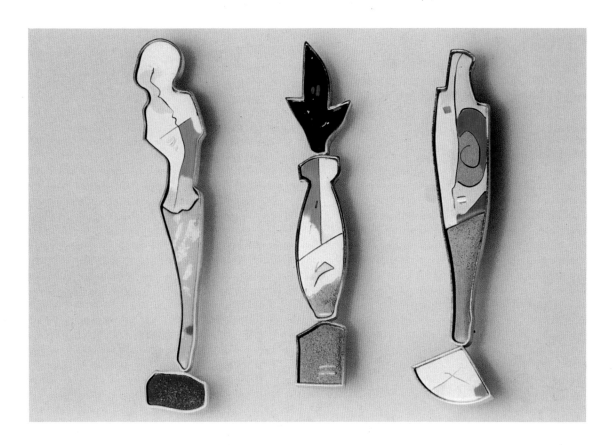

As the 1970s progressed, some jewelers began investigating a larger-scale format. There was also much experimentation with plastics. Albert Paley created grand, undulating neck pieces, made from copper, silver, gold, semiprecious stones, and the synthetic Delrin. Cara Lee Croninger (New York) cast primitivistic rocklike forms from hand-colored polyester resin and acrylic, which she then carved into tribal-looking bead necklaces and bracelets. Robert Lee Morris (New York) drew inspiration from ancient and ethnic sources for his sizable silver and/or brass neck pieces, bracelets, and rings, which often reflected contours of the body's bone structure.

In 1973, the Institute of Contemporary Art in Boston held a landmark exhibition, "Jewelry as Sculpture as Jewelry," in which works by Mitsukata, Croninger, and Morris were shown with jewelry designed by, among others, Pablo Picasso, Georges Braque, Roy Lichtenstein, and Man Ray. The impact was reminiscent of the 1946 exhibition at the Museum of Modern Art, which also combined jewelry by both craftspeople and painters and sculptors.

The 1970s also witnessed the exploration of metals not traditionally used in jewelry. Mary Ann Scherr (New York and later North Carolina) experimented with the possibilities inherent in steel, stainless steel, and aluminum. Scherr's experiments led to electronic "body monitors": jewelry engineered with medical equipment, such as tracheotomy tubes and electrocardiograms, which, with their inspired design and craftsmanship, made this equipment more acceptable to both medical users and those who viewed it.

Color, traditionally conveyed through stones and enamel, became a dominant theme in the 1970s. William Harper and Jamie Bennett were among the most important enamelists of the 1970s. Bennett is responsible for the extensive investigation of

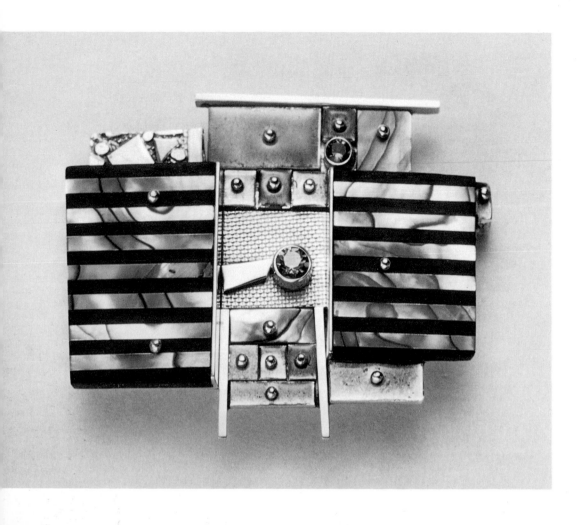

Earl Pardon. Brooch. 1984–86. Sterling silver, 14-karat gold, enamel, ivory, shell, gemstones. Constructed. 1½ x 1⅞ x ¼". Photograph: Courtesy Aaron Faber Gallery, New York

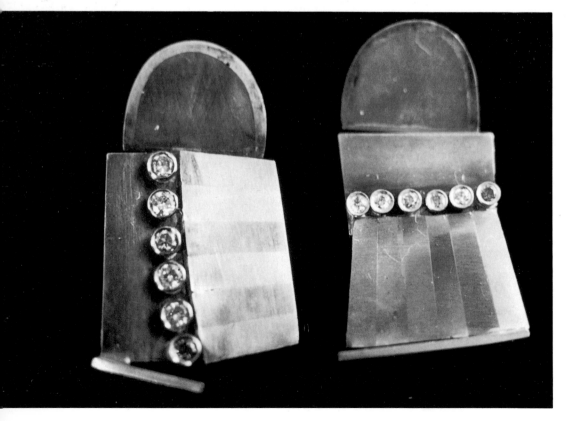

Glenda Arentzen. *Complementary Pair of Earrings.* 1975. Natural-colored diamonds, nickel, colored golds, patina. Fabricated nickel, gold alloys (some fabricated). 1¼ x ¾". Private collection. Photograph: Glenda Arentzen

matte enamel, while Harper explored the artistic possibilities of combining enamel-work with found objects. Earl Pardon's jewelry from the 1970s and early 1980s encompassed complex constructions of enameled copper "chips" and colored beads, combined with metal. A more subtle approach to color was seen in the jewelry of Glenda Arentzen, a former student of Pardon's at Skidmore College in Saratoga Springs, New York. Arentzen utilized the marriage of metals technique, possibly developed by the Castillo brothers in Taxco, Mexico; it combined metals such as silver with copper, brass, and nickel to achieve subtly colored surface patterning.

By the mid-1970s, many jewelers turned to the color possibilities inherent in refractory metals. Refractory metals include titanium, tantalum, and niobium, all of which change color when exposed to specific electric currents while immersed in an electrolytic solution. Aluminum, which can be effectively anodized as well, was also used.

Helen Shirk. Bracelet. 1975. Silver, brass, Delrin, hematites. 4 x 4"

Helen Shirk (California) another student of Pardon's from Skidmore College (as well as Alma Eikerman's at Indiana University), created complex three-dimensional structures using color. Her pieces from the late 1970s incorporated silver, brass, gold, and copper with plastic and opaque semiprecious stones. In the early 1980s, Shirk began to emphasize line rather than volume in her work and to achieve color accents with titanium, as its inherent strength allowed for structurally strong and thin colored lines.

The jewelry of Florence Resnikoff (California) reads like a history of color techniques. She explored color with patinas in the 1950s, dyed and cast resins in the 1960s, patinated electroplating, metal and stone inlays, and *mokume-gane* in the 1970s, and refractory metals in the 1980s.

David Tisdale (New York) pioneered the use of anodized aluminum, a process he brought from industry to the metals studio. Although, like Helen Shirk, he currently finds expression in hollowware (and in Tisdale's case, additionally in flatware), he made much jewelry in the early 1980s, both one-of-a-kind and production. Inspired by the clean lines and angles of architecture, Tisdale adapted the repetition of doors, windows, and arches to his geometric and colorful jewelry. He often included other materials, such as plastic, precious and semiprecious stones, or wood, with the anodized aluminum.

54

The 1970s and early 1980s was a pluralistic period in jewelry. Diametrically opposite to the abstract, hard-edge aesthetic of David Tisdale was the mannerist imagery of Richard Mawdsley (Carbondale, Illinois). Mawdsley's neck pieces show fantastic worlds populated with Medusa-like heads and phantasmagorical creatures. He created entire environments on bracelets, complete with tiny, precision-crafted chalices, plates, and flatware. Mawdsley fabricated these pieces from gold, silver, stones, and refractory metals.

The mid-twentieth century was a time of revolution and growth with regard to form, technology, and concept in modern jewelry. There was a tremendous amount of cross-pollination among artists, who willingly shared inventions, methods, discoveries, techniques, and perhaps most important, conceptual orientations. It was also a time of new and imaginative explorations of materials suitable for jewelry. One of the most exciting aspects of the best jewelry made between 1940 and 1980 was its innovation—not only in its combinations of atypical materials for jewelry but also in the jewelers' sheer desire to explore the greatest possible variety of things.

One artist who has pioneered, invented, and manipulated an immense array of materials is Thomas Gentille (New York). He was trained as a painter and sculptor beginning in 1957, graduating from Cleveland Institute of Art, where he studied with John Paul Miller. Gentille was among the first artists to explore unusual materials, which he felt were applicable to jewelry because of their inherent beauty. His work is

David Tisdale. Neck piece. 1981. Anodized aluminum, sterling silver, diamonds. Fabricated. 1¹/₂ x 7 x 5¹/₂″. Collection Helen W. Drutt English, Philadelphia. Photograph: Craig Clifford

about form and structure and is interpreted through the pristine use of diverse substances like bronze, alabaster, eggshell, wood, fiber, anodized aluminum, plastics, pure pigments, and gold. Displaying no favoritism toward any particular material or group of materials, Gentille investigates each for its unique properties, harmonic and disharmonic relationships and juxtapositions, and permanence.

William Harper (Tallahassee, Florida), also a graduate of Cleveland Institute of Art, spent his formative years in the 1970s. His pendants and brooches express his own amalgam of primitive and Judeo-Christian iconography. His masterful enameling technique is used to an irreverent end, and, a maximalist, Harper employs an eclectic variety of materials that appeal to him, frequently including found objects. His jewelry might combine richly enameled portions, mounted in gold frames, with shells, precious and semiprecious stones, and detritus such as broken bicycle reflectors, pig's teeth, or animal vertebrae. He selects these objects for their aesthetic qualities and the symbolism they might add to his narrative.

Harper picked up, some ten years later, where Sam Kramer left off when he died in 1964. This continuation was not necessarily conscious on Harper's part, but both he and Sam Kramer have made their audiences look within themselves and at their dreams and visions, toward worlds that exist in their collective fantasies.

On the other side of the spectrum, the analytical constructivism of Margaret de Patta has reemerged circa 1980 in the jewelry of Eleanor Moty (Madison, Wisconsin) and Deborah Aguado (New York). They both form satisfying architectonic constructions in which the gemstones and metal are married in perfect harmony, with the gold mountings complementing the facets and inclusions within the stones. Moty's work is more directly in the line of de Patta, whereas Aguado often breaks away from these concerns.

"Good as Gold," a traveling exhibition organized by SITES (Smithsonian Institution Traveling Exhibition Service) in 1981, showed the many alternatives then being explored by artists in contrast to the traditional jewelry materials of precious metals and gemstones with which the public was more familiar. The exhibition was pivotal in that it demonstrated this phenomenon to other artists working in a variety of fields, as well as to the general public.

All in all, we have come full circle from the nascence of what some now call American art jewelry. From its seminal beginning around 1940 into the early 1980s, American jewelry had never been so rich in technical expertise, material diversity, formal innovation, and sheer energy, laying the foundation for the superb jewelers who were to follow.

NOTES:
1. See Deborah Norton, "A History of the School for American Craftsmen," *Metalsmith* 5, no. 1 (Winter 1985): 16.
2. See Toni Lesser Wolf, "Ed Wiener," in *Design 1935–1965: What Modern Was*, ed. Martin Eidelberg (New York: Harry N. Abrams, 1991), 252.
3. See Robert Cardinale and Hazel Bray, "Margaret de Patta: Structure, Concepts and Design Sources," *Metalsmith* 3, no. 2 (Spring 1983): 12.
4. See Yoshiko Uchida, "Margaret de Patta," in *The Jewelry of Margaret de Patta*, exhib. cat. (Oakland: The Oakes Gallery and The Oakland Museum, 1976), 15.
5. See Michael Dunas, "Funk Art Jewelry: Ken Cory and the Pencil Bros," *Metalsmith* 8, no. 2 (Spring 1988): 17.
6. See Alma Eikerman, *Objects: U.S.A.* (New York: Viking Press, 1970), 197.
7. Fred Fenster, letter to Susan Grant Lewin, 10 August 1989.
8. See Robert Cardinale, "A Decade of Metalsmithing in the United States, 1970–1980," *Metalsmith* 1, no. 1 (Fall 1980): 23.

opposite: Thomas Gentille. Pin. 1964. Green gold, inlaid peacock feathers. Approx. 2½ x 2½". Whereabouts unknown

The Power of the Intimate:
On Contemporary Jewelry and Sculpture

SUZANNE RAMLJAK

above: Joseph Cornell. *Untitled (Apollinaris).* c. 1953. Box construction. 19 x 11 x 5"

opposite: Keith E. Lo Bue. *Where Music Dwells.* Pendant. 1993. Found objects, text. Assembled. Diam. 2 x ½". Collection Toni Greenbaum, New York. Photograph: Keith Lo Bue

This book could just as aptly have been subtitled *American Small-Scale Sculpture* instead of *American Art Jewelry Today.* The dividing line between jewelry and sculpture is largely an imaginary one. Size notwithstanding, the world of the jeweler is the world of the sculptor; they partake of the same rich cultural heritage and face the same aesthetic and material challenges. Proof of this kinship can be found in their many shared qualities and concerns.

Early developments in twentieth-century art continue to shape both contemporary jewelry and sculpture. Assemblage in particular has irreversibly changed three-dimensional art, rivaling modeling or fabrication as the prime sculptural method. Joseph Cornell, a master of early assemblage, has direct descendants in contemporary jewelry, most notably Thomas Mann, Keith E. LoBue, and Robin Kranitzky and Kim Overstreet. A preoccupation with formal means that marked the first half of this century also prevails in the art of today. The technical mastery involved in creating small objects has made jewelers especially attentive to the properties and possibilities of materials.

Artistic movements since 1960—Pop art, Minimalism, environmental art, public art, appropriation—have all found reception in the work of contemporary jewelers. Even the latest sculptural trends—site specificity and interactivity, which aim to actively engage the viewer—play a key role in today's jewelry.

In the late 1980s and early 1990s, numerous projects were organized under the heading of site specificity. Site-specific projects attempt to respond directly to the physical and cultural conditions of a site, accommodating and extending those conditions. Jewelry has always had a legitimate claim to site specificity; it is designed specifically for the human body, which can be likened to an exhibition space or portable gallery on which objects are displayed. Jewelry is thus always *in situ* on the human body—its site could not be more specific. The term *jewelry* does not adequately convey this crucial link between wearer and work. Though also problematic, *ornament* comes closer to suggesting the bodily dependence of jewelry.

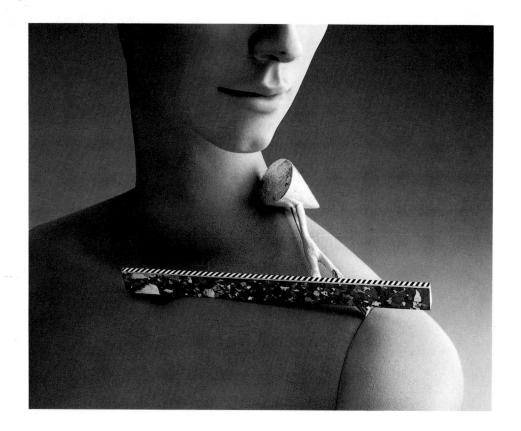

Leslie Leupp. *Internal Bleeding #1.*
Brooch. 1986. Wood, linoleum, paint, silver leaf. Fabricated. 3½ x 8 x 1½". Collection Rachelle Thiewes, El Paso. Photograph: Robert Suddarth

While all jewelers must come to terms with the human site, two artists who consciously grapple with the limits and demands of the body are Arline Fisch and Leslie Leupp. Leupp cultivates tensions within the work's structure and between the work and the wearer. Approaching the body as an active object in the round rather than a flat surface for attaching objects, he adds new angles and shapes to the human form. Arline Fisch explores what she calls "human scale" or "body scale" rather than the intimate scale of most jewelry. She often makes collars or breastplates, armorlike structures that relate to the architecture of the human form.

Marjorie Schick's explorations of the body have resulted in some of the most extravagant and encompassing structures for the human form. An engineering tour de force, her construction works virtually envelop the wearer in a material cocoon. These challenging works totally redefine the contours of the human frame. Schick's constructions have a marked affinity with the most ambitious site-specific sculpture being done today, such as Tadashi Kawamata's 1992 *Project on Roosevelt Island* in New York, a series of wood scaffolds surrounding the island's abandoned architecture.

Interactive art is another prime area of exploration in both contemporary sculpture and jewelry. Many large-scale works solicit viewer involvement, inviting or requiring them to move and manipulate sculptural elements. The goal is to turn the viewer into a participant, from a passive witness into an active partner. The most involving and technologically complex artistic experience, virtual reality, simulates bodily transport into an artificial realm. However, all such experiences remain virtual, at one remove from the world. Jewelry, on the other hand, provides a direct interactive experience. Placing an object on the body elicits an immediate response, demanding adjustment of movement or pose. With jewelry, the viewer has no choice but to adapt and respond to the material object, and this response—unlike a momentary encounter with an interactive sculptural environment—continues as long as the piece remains on the body.

opposite above: Tadashi Kawamata. *Kawamata Project on Roosevelt Island.* 1992. Photograph: on the table, inc.

opposite below left: Arline Fisch. Halter and skirt. 1968. Halter: sterling silver. Hammered and fabricated. 11 x 22". Skirt: printed velvet by Jack Lenor Larsen. 24 x 46". Collection American Craft Museum. Photograph: Ferdinand Bosch

opposite below right: Marjorie Schick. Folding body sculpture. 1987. Painted wood, reed, cord. 96 x 22 x 1½". Model: Beth Neubert. Photograph: Gary Pollmiller

Sandra Sherman. Bracelet. 1988. Sterling silver. Constructed. Diam. 5 x ¼″ (flat). Photograph: Jochen Grün

opposite: Rachelle Thiewes. *Silent Dance Series.* Brooch. 1990. Silver, 18-karat gold. Heat, chemical color on photographic image. 40 x 30 x 2″. Collection the artist. Photograph: Rachelle Thiewes

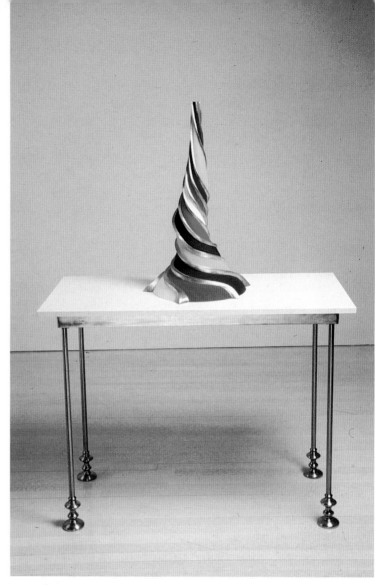

Each jeweler requests different degrees of wearer interaction and participation. Sandra Sherman's kinetic pieces change structure and volume in response to wearer movement, setting up a symbiotic relationship. Boris Bally's works, among the most demanding of today's art jewelry, require a special commitment, as they nearly para-lyze the wearer's limbs. The highly wearer-responsive jewelry of Rachelle Thiewes calls for attention and intelligence; her sharp forms prod the wearers into conscious-ness and remind them that their actions have consequences.

Yet another key area of sculptural activity is public art. It can be argued that all jewelry is a form of public art. Acting as a physical billboard, the wearer takes a private statement out into public every day. Admittedly, jewelry is not permanently sited in public or commissioned by a group, like most public art. People cannot walk through it or rest on it. Instead, they walk toward it and draw near to get the mes-sage.

Jewelry's ability to deliver a public message is demonstrated by the work of Joyce Scott. Scott enlists her formidable skill and dazzling beadwork to address a range of subjects including slavery, social injustice, sexual abuse, and the Holocaust. The work's message becomes even more striking when delivered at close range around a wearer's neck. Such heated jewelry gives new meaning to the expression "in your face."

The many other functions that art performs—providing pleasure, education, commemoration, play—jewelry also fufills. Even the most sophisticated philosophical issues can be addressed in this format. Myra Mimlitsch-Gray's highly critical work is a case in point. Her diamond-studded pendants offer a reevaluation of this precious stone and affirm the ontological premise that identity or being is the result of function, not essence. Joan Parcher's graphite pendulums also operate on a conceptual plane. The wearer's motions are registered by the graphite marks, providing a graphic demonstration of causality and an existential reminder of our actions.

Mimlitsch-Gray and Parcher's works are on a par, visually and conceptually, with those of contemporary German sculptor Rebecca Horn, whose quirky, mechanized contraptions, laden with alchemical connotations, appear strangely animated. This conceptual strain is more prominent in European than American jewelry, and it is fitting that the work of Parcher and Gray most resemble the work of a European artist.

Playfulness and sensual delight are more characteristic of contemporary American jewelry than of the theory- and design-oriented jewelry of Europe. Daniel Jocz's richly pigmented and textured forms relate closely to the virtuoso effects of sculptor Saint Clair Cemin. In a more playful vein, Barbara Walter makes punning rings bearing titles like *Gopher Broke, Wheel of Fortune Ring Toy*. These amusing finger toys can be compared with the large-scale public projects of an artist like Tom Otterness, who creates clever and humorous scenarios with cartoonlike figures.

Beyond the similarities between contemporary jewelry and sculpture, jewelry has unique attributes tied to its intimate engagement with the body. The power of this intimacy cannot be overstated; it is a power based on the sense of touch. More essential than sight, smell, hearing, or taste, touch is the only one of our senses without which we cannot live. Touch has the power to heal, to arouse, to bring to life. Essential as it is, few socially sanctioned opportunities exist to indulge this sense. The touch of jewelry serves as a quiet arousal, a type of foreplay for the larger sensations of life.

Jewelry is the only art form that provides this direct contact with the body. Though we may speak of tactility in relation to sculpture, the touch is usually vicarious. We almost invariably experience sculpture visually, not tactilely. While sculpture's vicarious touch sets it at a remove from physical contact with the human body, jewelry is endowed with the irresistible force of direct touch.

Besides touch, jewelry's other key asset is its small scale, its captivating intimacy. One can put a twist on the maxim "less is more" and claim that "small is big," or that smallness has large implications. This constitutes a reversal of our normal values, which hold that big is powerful: "the bigger the better." By extension, we have come to believe that public events are more significant than private encounters. The opposite proves to be true. What happens in private, behind closed doors, shapes us in potent ways. Family interaction, a mother's love carry more weight than any government program. It is in the small spaces, the intimate exchanges, the details that real feelings transpire. The words expressed in whispers can drown out the roar of a crowd.

Fortunately, we need not choose between public and private, between elaborate environments or small, engaging objects, between sculpture and jewelry. Both have the power to affect us. We simply have to keep our senses open to their appeals for our attention.

Portfolio of Jewelry Artists

Deborah Aguado

Unlike many contemporary jewelers, Deborah Aguado does not shun precious stones. Instead, she has set herself the challenge of designing new settings and compositions for these old but noble materials. In her quest to make traditional gemstones interesting she is drawn to what she calls "fantasy" or "free" cut stones with complex and irregular faceting.* She counters the gem's ephemeral and dazzling light effects with strongly engineered metal compositions. Her interest in engineering or architectonic structure is implied by series titles such as Facades, Night Trains and Hoists. The works in the Hoist series actually include elements that are suspended within the brooch.

Since 1984 the artist has used her considerable skill to explore more personal and rural concerns. Her series called Tokonoma is a response to the death of her mother during the season of spring. The materials incorporated in this series, such as twigs and ground cover, all allude to the changing of seasons and loss. Like the earlier works that sought to contain the unbound nature of light, this series attempts to contain the unbound nature of grief. In the artist's own words, these works "guard against the darkness, the cold of winter, the snow of death."

* All quotations from artists in the following pages come from information gathered by the author in interviews, letters, and other personal communications.

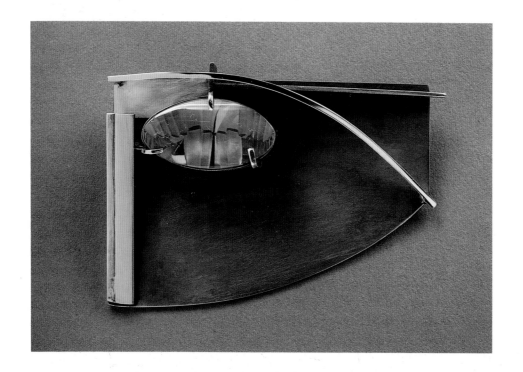

left: Deborah Aguado. *Idols Eye I.* From the Hoist series. Pin. 1989. Sterling silver, citrine, 18-karat gold. Constructed. 2$^{1}/_{4}$ x 3$^{1}/_{2}$ x $^{1}/_{2}$". Collection the artist. Design © Deborah Aguado. Photograph: Bobby Hansson

opposite: Deborah Aguado. Five pins from the Tokonoma series. 1985. Sterling silver, twigs, bark, acorn caps, dentritic agate. Constructed. Each 3 x 1$^{1}/_{4}$ x $^{1}/_{2}$". Collection the artist and private collections. Design © Deborah Aguado. Photograph: Bobby Hansson

Amy Anthony

Amy Anthony's tool-and-die training is seminal to her work, and she uses professional milling machines, lathes, and drill presses to achieve a cool, machined look. Like the Minimalist sculptures of Donald Judd, these works have smooth, perfect surfaces without impurities. Nonetheless, Anthony's small works are quite wearer-friendly.

Anthony refers to her steel and aluminum works as drawings, and they do share with drawings a graphite grayness and two dimensionality. But while Anthony's works are planar and concerned with surface patterns, they ultimately go beyond two dimensions to address the fourth dimension—time. The play of reflective light suggests time through motion, and the artist makes repeated reference to the stability and inert physical composition of the metals she enlists. Thus, Anthony's seemingly simple "drawings" and self-effacing technique engage complex issues of time and imperceptible change.

left: Amy Anthony. Brooch. 1988. Aluminum, steel. Machined, anodized, drilled, tapped. $^3/_8$ x $^3/_4$ x $^1/_8$". Photograph: Woody Packard

opposite: Amy Anthony. Brooch. 1991. Aluminum, stainless steel. Stainless steel roll pins for bonding. $1^1/_2$ x 1 x $^3/_8$". Photograph: Woody Packard

Boris Bally

During his youth, Boris Bally was fascinated by weaponry and would draw and design weapons of his own. In later years, he went on to work in industrial design and model making. Machinery continues to inspire Bally's jewelry, and he still scrounges for inspiration in the scrap yards of Pittsburgh, where he finds discarded robotic parts from nearby Carnegie-Mellon Institute.

Bally has translated his interest in unfriendly machinery into engaging works that make intimate claims on the wearer. While their machinelike precision and clinical perfection give his works a dangerous and threatening edge, they draw the viewer in with intriguing construction and precious stones like rubies.

Bally's *Constrictor* is a perfect example of this mixed aesthetic. It is a tour de force of metal fabrication, combining sterling silver, rubies, brass, and titanium with springs, rivets, and tubes. The circular composition, nearly a foot in diameter, holds three syringe structures that press against the arm like the clamps of a delicate vise. The overall effect is similar to a medical contraption, setting the arm in traction and debilitating the wearer.

The look of high technology and feeling of entrapment offer a challenge for the wearer and viewer of Bally's works. As the artist states, "It takes more guts to put something of mine on." Not only are his large-scale pieces a challenge to wear, they also demand time and effort to put on, often requiring an assistant. By placing such demands on wearers, Bally's works help to invigorate their relationship with contemporary jewelry.

opposite above: Boris Bally. *Directional Triarcs.* Shirt form. 1990. Sterling silver, oxidized copper, brass pins, brass springs. Metal marriage with copper, fabricated silver, forge-printed, roll-printed. 3 x 10 x ¹/₄″. Collection the artist. Photograph: David L. Smith

opposite below: Boris Bally. *Constrictor.* Arm form. 1990. Sterling silver, rubies, oxidized brass, anodized titanium, stainless steel springs. Fabricated silver, tube settings, cold jointing, rivets, twist joints. 2 x 11 x 11″, expanding to 2 x 12¹/₂ x 12¹/₂″. Collection the artist. Photograph: David L. Smith

left: Boris Bally. *Eat Wear.* Bracelets, ring, flatware. 1992. Gold-plated brass, sterling silver. Fabricated brass, file texture, cast and polished sterling silver, rivets. 10¹/₂ x 11 x 1¹/₂″. Collection Arrowmont School of Crafts, Gatlinburg, and the artist. Photograph: Dean Powell

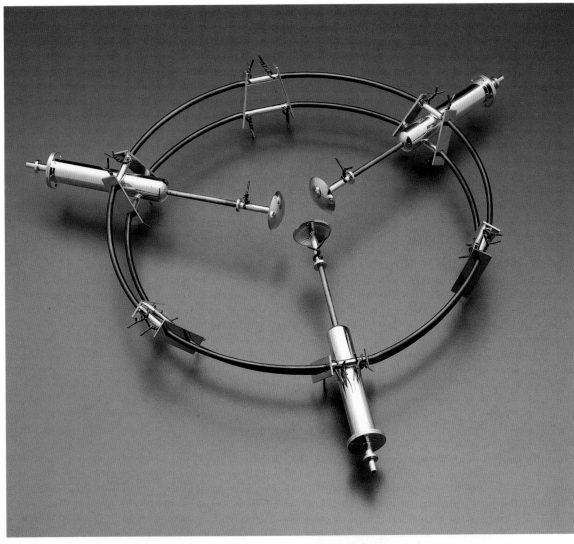

Rebecca Batal

In addition to jewelry, Rebecca Batal also creates poetry. In the same way that poets keep language alive and fresh, jewelers keep our bodies alive and alert. Batal sees jewelry as a "charm" that keeps us awake and enlivens those in need of "respiration." Adornment serves as a constant reminder of the body, arousing our physical awareness.

Batal's poetic background is conveyed in the surreal and evocative imagery of her works. Often sparse, they are more like haiku poems than sonnets. A case in point is an untitled clip of 1990 that combines the resonant elements of ladder and slide, one climbing upward and the other suggesting quick descent. If worn on a pocket, only one side of the clip is revealed, leading the eye, and the imagination, into the clothes of the wearer.

Batal's works unite contrasting, even irreconcilable elements, producing a spark to rekindle both the body and the imagination. *Medal of Honor* combines a cap gun with baby pink and blue ribbons. A trident-shaped pin is covered in seed pearls; the sharp-pronged weapon is made to seem precious, even cute. Like the Surrealists, Batal creates subtly disquieting objects. Though they are often beautiful, it is a "convulsive" Surrealist beauty rather than the serene beauty of classicism.

below left: Rebecca Batal. Clip. 1990. 18-karat gold. Constructed. 3 x ¼ x ½". Photograph: Roger Birn

below right: Rebecca Batal. *Medal of Honor.* Pendant. 1989. Cap gun, ribbon. Constructed. Pendant 4½ x 2 x ¾", ribbons 36". Photograph: John Rose

opposite: Rebecca Batal. *Chopin Pendant.* 1989. Crystal beads, hematite, plaster, found object. Constructed. Collection Helen W. Drutt English. Photograph: Jack Ramsdale

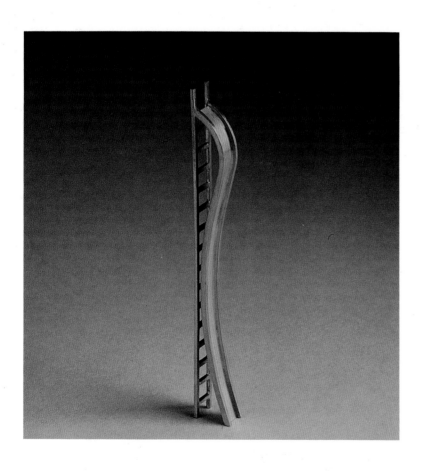

Jamie Bennett

Throughout his career, Jamie Bennett has sought to attain the unification of color and form. Bennett began as a painter and became attracted to sculptural form because it was not constrained, like painting, to a rectangular frame. His early three-dimensional work was marked by gestural surface effects and nonillusional pictorial effects, and he later turned to more sculptural forms.

Though three-dimensional art is not typically marked by vivid color, with most sculptors and jewelers opting for subdued or monochrome works, Bennett has set out to work in the mode of colored sculpture. Matte enamel has become Bennett's preferred medium for this exploration, and in his experimentation, he has electroformed it in ways never before achieved. Through the physical properties of enamel, its potential as pure color and form, Bennett has sought to make his color intrinsic to his work's structure.

Bennett's completed works often look like feathers or stafflike markers on the body. These vertical staffs can be worn in groups or spaced on the body like mile markers or landmarks. Bennett's small, integral objects are designed to be sympathetic to the wearer. In the same way that color and form merge within the piece, the work becomes one with the wearer.

opposite above: Jamie Bennett. *Chroma 3.* Brooch. 1991. Enamel on copper. Electroformed, enameled. $1^{1}/_{2}$ x $4^{1}/_{2}$ x $^{3}/_{8}$". Collection the artist. Photograph: John Lenz

opposite below left: Jamie Bennett. *Rocaille 14.* Brooch. 1992. Enamel on copper, 22-, 24-, and 14-karat gold. Electroformed, enameled, fabricated gold. 6 x $2^{1}/_{4}$ x $^{1}/_{2}$". Private collection. Photograph: John Lenz

opposite below right: Jamie Bennett. *Rocaille 13.* Brooch. 1992. Enamel on copper, 22- and 14-karat gold. Electroformed, enameled, fabricated gold. 5 x 2 x $^{1}/_{2}$". Collection the artist. Photograph: John Lenz

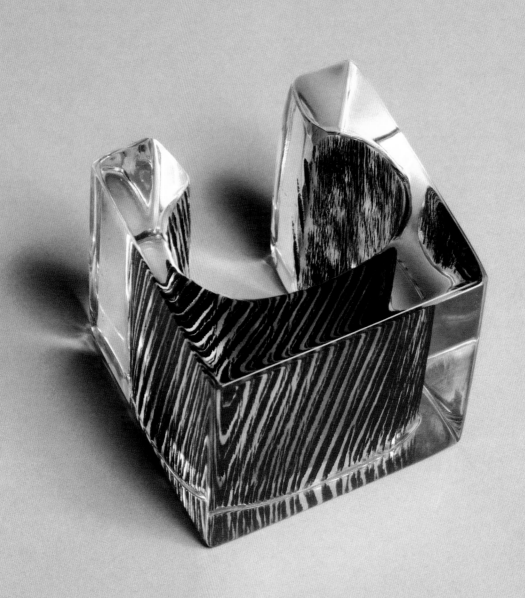

Cara Lee Croninger

Cara Lee Croninger's work manages to redeem one of the least appealing and least popular of modern materials: plastic. As the artist acknowledges, "Plastic has such a bad reputation." Preferring to work in cast polyester resins and acrylics, Croninger is one of the few artists who have successfully transformed these materials into engaging works of wearable art. These synthetic materials are further "tamed" by the inclusion of organic materials like leather string.

Though Croninger begins with manmade or synthetic materials, the results are anything but artificial. With the skills she has developed working with these unnatural materials, especially resin, she has molded them into sensuously organic shapes, creating forms that have all the subtlety of minerals or the juiciness of citrus fruits, and endowed them with rich, radiant hues.

The scale and assertive volumes of some of her works may cause a degree of awkward movement on the part of wearers, but what they lose in easy movement they gain in bold color and luminously engaging forms.

right: Cara Lee Croninger. *Polyester Bangle.* 1989. Polyester resin. Hand-cast, colored, carved. Diam. 4¹/₂ x 2″. Private collection. Photograph: Hugh Bell

opposite: Cara Lee Croninger. *Clear Acrylic Cuff.* 1988. Acrylic. Carved, stained. 3 x 3 x 3″. Private collection. Photograph: Hugh Bell

Claire A. Dinsmore

Like many jewelers, Claire Dinsmore is drawn to the intimacy and personal involvement that jewelry's small scale provides. Dinsmore began her art studies as a ceramist and discovered that large-scale sculpture created distance or anonymity between the viewer and object, a distance that is bridged in the process of wearing a piece of jewelry.

The artist's personal involvement with her works can be sensed in their precision and delightfully engaging detail. To achieve a finished construction, Dinsmore employs multiple metalsmithing processes, including cutting, filing, drilling, soldering, sandblasting, and anodizing. Several of the pieces also use small nuts and bolts, which become incorporated into the design as compositional elements. A strong sense of depth is suggested by the layering of materials and the linear demarcation of space. Though Dinsmore has chosen to work in small scale, her earrings and pins are actually quite large-scale in the world of jewelry, and they partake of the spatial dynamics of large sculpture.

opposite: Claire A. Dinsmore. *Bracelet #1.* From the Kokoro Series. 1987. Sterling silver, anodized aluminum, plated tubes, nuts, bolts. Constructed. $3^3/_8$ x $3^1/_4$ x $^1/_2$". Collection Helen W. Drutt English, Philadelphia. Photograph: Ralph Gabriner

overleaf left: Claire A. Dinsmore. *Release (The Power of Freedom).* Necklace. 1990. Sterling silver, Berlin Wall shard, ColorCore. Constructed. $4^1/_2$ x 1 x $^1/_2$". Private collection. Photograph: Ralph Gabriner

overleaf above right: Claire A. Dinsmore. *Support Series Brooch #3.* 1991. Sterling silver, ColorCore, Surell. Fabricated, carved. 3 x 1 x $^1/_2$". Collection Virginia Bower, Princeton, N.J. Photograph: Ralph Gabriner

overleaf below right: Claire A. Dinsmore. *Bracelet #2.* From the Sympathetic series. 1992. Sterling silver, Surell. Fabricated, carved. $3^1/_2$ x 4 x $^7/_{16}$". Courtesy Helen Drutt Gallery, Philadelphia. Photograph: Ralph Gabriner

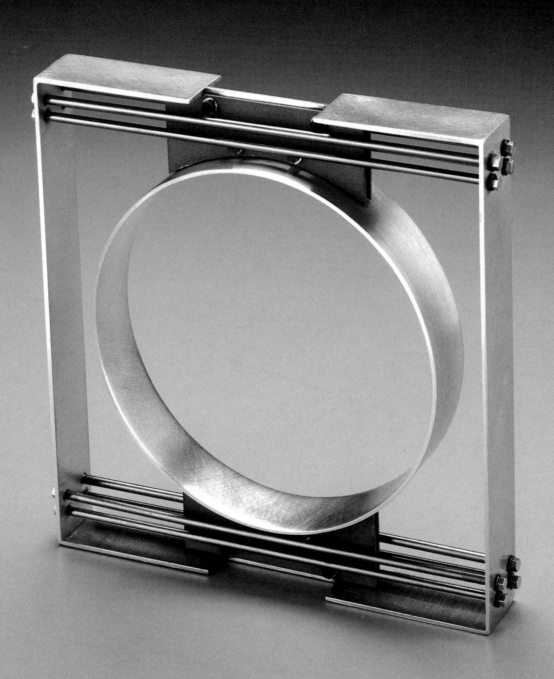

Robert W. Ebendorf

Robert Ebendorf takes an unbridled, almost childlike, joy in all forms. This polymorphous delight is contrasted with the limited sources of pleasure we are allowed as adults. Ebendorf's work visually preserves our earlier delight.

Ebendorf acknowledges that his work is motivated by an active curiosity and love of the material world. "I think my work has always had the quality of questioning, of investigation," he says. This restless inquiry is in turn fueled by Ebendorf's energy and unrelenting desire to make and transform things.

Ebendorf has naturally been drawn to the artistic technique that employs the greatest diversity of forms, namely collage. Collage is the inclusive technique par excellence. While many jewelers employ collage today, Ebendorf was one of the first to exploit it, and he now practices it with vitality and confidence. This bold facility applies to both materials—everything from Korean newspapers to shattered windshield glass—and the range of references, from Christianity to pop culture.

Ebendorf's career reads like a dictionary of possibilities. Indeed, his work illustrates the most liberating idea of all: anything is possible. Ebendorf's artistic license is contagious, and he has infected an entire generation of young, innovative jewelers.

opposite above: Robert W. Ebendorf. *Cross Brooch.* 1992. Broken glass, beach glass, LP record. Constructed. $1^1/_2$ x 3 x $1^1/_2$". Collection the artist. Photograph: Jim Cummins Studio, courtesy Susan Cummins Gallery

opposite below: Robert W. Ebendorf. *Collar.* 1988. Chinese paper, 24-carat gold, foil, wood, Plexiglas. Constructed. Diam. $11^7/_8$". Collection The Society for Art in Crafts, Pittsburgh. Photograph: T. Nakamura

Robert W. Ebendorf. *Collar.* 1984. Color-Core, rubber cord, sterling silver. Constructed. Diam. 11⁷/₈″. Collection D. Schneier, New York. Photograph: T. Nakamura

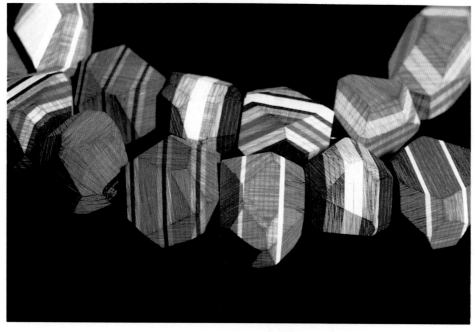

Robert W. Ebendorf. *Necklace* (detail). 1987. Layered ColorCore. Constructed. Diam. 9⁷/₈″. Collection The Art Institute of Chicago. American Arts Collection. Photograph: T. Nakamura

Robert W. Ebendorf. *Mixed Media Necklace.* 1988. Seashell, bone, gold foil, blue cut glass, beach pebbles, slate, old photographs, postage stamps, ColorCore, Japanese handmade paper, niobium. Constructed. Each bead average diam. 2″. Collection D. Schneier, New York. Photograph: Noel Allum Photography

Eva Eisler

Eva Eisler's conceptual and constructivist works enjoin a European sensibility—not surprisingly, as she was born and schooled in Czechoslovakia. The artist refers to her jewelry as a "visual object or tool that expresses my philosophy." The basic tenets of that philosophy are logic, order, simplicity, and freedom, all expressed with natural materials and techniques.

The works that result from her philosophy are highly linear and planar constructions held together in states of tension, like bridge spans. The artist even produced a series under the title Tensions. This interest in tension, and in the dynamics of compression and friction, no doubt stems from Eisler's early training in architecture. Eisler's architectural background also taught her strict discipline and the skills to construct complex objects that can be dismantled and reassembled.

Eisler's commitment to geometry and strict form is tied to her concern for the effects of technology and our muddled relationship to our environment. Relying on the truth that people find comfort in order, Eisler attempts to lay bare the logic and conceptual order of our world through the order and purity in her work. Its intellectual and structural purity provides a sense of well-being and security that comes from any well-ordered composition.

opposite: Eva Eisler. *Tension Series II.* Brooch. 1990. Sterling silver, slate. Cold connection constructed. 5 x 3 x ½". Private collection. Photograph: George Erml

below: Eva Eisler. *Tension Series V.* Brooch. 1992. Sterling silver, stainless steel. Cold connection constructed, under tension. 2½ x 4½ x ½". Private collection. Photograph: George Erml

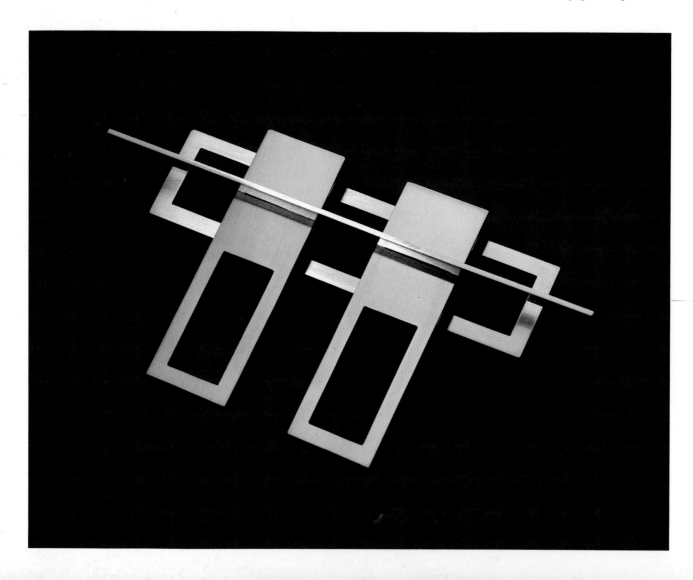

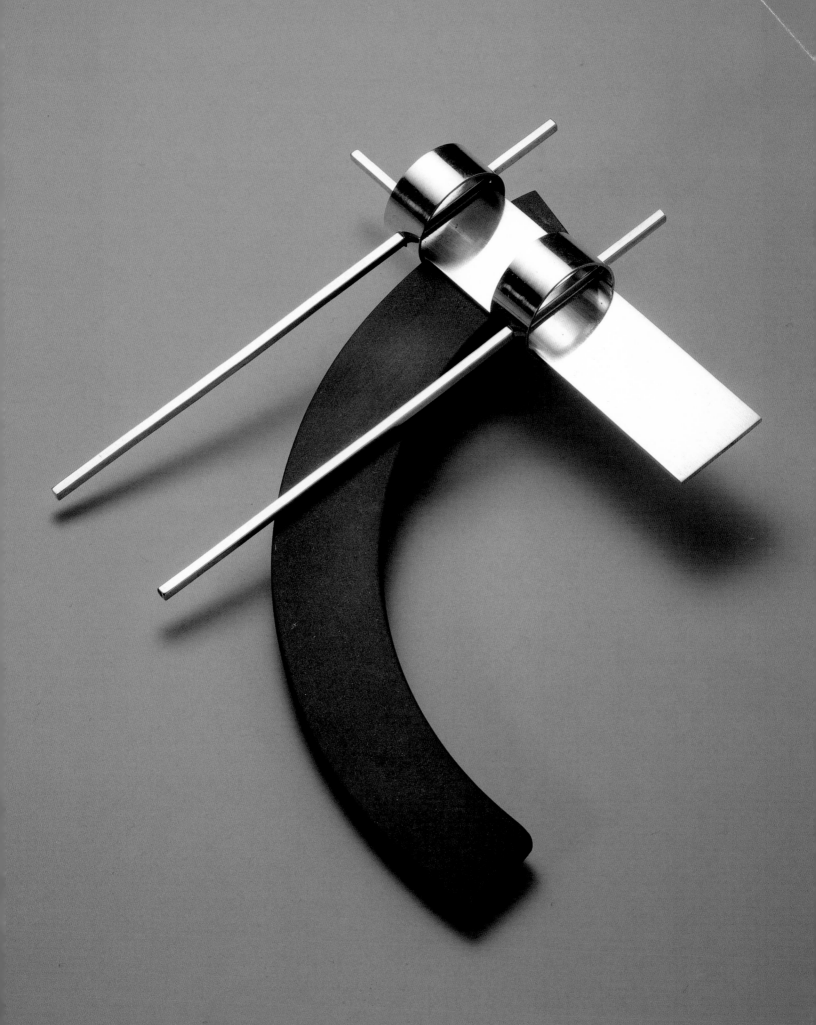

above: Eva Eisler. *Repose.* Three brooches. 1988. Slate, cut out and polished. Above to below, 2¼ x 3 x ¼"; 1½ x 4 x ¼"; 1½ x 5 x ¼". Private collection. Photograph: George Erml

opposite: Eva Eisler. Brooch. 1989. Sterling silver. Cold connection constructed, under tension. ¾ x 5 x ¾". Private collection. Photograph: George Erml

90

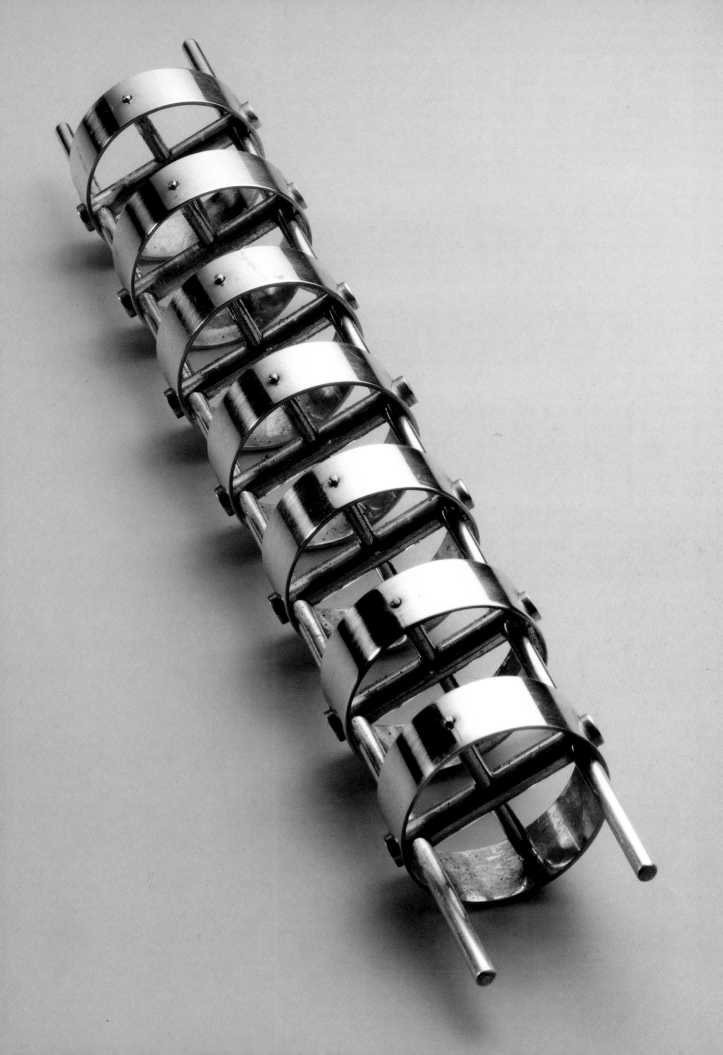

Sandra Enterline

Sandra Enterline takes the hard forms and materials of industry and renders them surprisingly soft and sensual. Enterline has said, "I have a sentimental urge . . . to reaccess the beauty of the industrial form." She expresses this beauty by giving a soft, warm finish to her forms through sanded or brushed surfaces. The hardness of the form is also alleviated through the use of patinas.

Enterline's preferred format, the pendant, also encourages a tactile engagement. Dangling on the neck, these objects ask to be touched and fondled, not just looked at. Her hollow forms swell and curve in an inviting manner. Further interest is created through incised openings or the inclusion of small objects like ball bearings. Though seemingly simple, Enterline's works have rich textural values and a complex play between interior and exterior.

Even in pieces that incorporate movement or sound, the effect is never loud. Enterline's work is eminently quiet and understated, marked by subtle nuances of white on white, nickel on silver. Like a whisper, they attract attention by their quiet self-restraint and hushed invitation.

Arline Fisch

Arline Fisch literally wrote the book on woven metal, and her *Textile Techniques in Metal for Jewelers* remains the authoritative book on the subject. Fisch has applied the ancient technique of weaving to the age-old materials of silver and gold to produce boldly contemporary works. According to the artist, ancient cultures provide her with "technical knowledge" and "design courage," both of which are amply evident in her captivating works.

Fisch has achieved the dexterity to handle gold like cloth, folding and pleating and fluting the woven metal swatches. These "pliable planes" give her remarkable flexibility to mold her shapes to the contours and movements of the human body. Fisch's concern for relating to the human body has led her to work in human or body scale rather than in the more intimate scale of most jewelers.

Many works even go beyond the scale of the body; larger-than-life-size pieces serve as dramatic extensions of the wearer's body and dress. Collars or breastplates rest on the body like protective armor, while others zigzag or project from the body like lively attachments. Winglike forms often recur in Fisch's work, bringing with them the optimistic associations of flight and liberty. Fisch considers her mission as a jeweler to "please and exalt the wearer."

below: Arline Fisch. *Double Collar.* Two necklaces. 1988. 18-karat gold, oxidized fine silver, hematite beads. Hand-knit construction. 3½ x 12 x 12″. Private collection. Photograph: William Gullette

opposite above: Arline Fisch. *Slit Twill Square.* Pendant. 1991. Oxidized sterling silver, 18-karat gold, onyx, hematite. Plaited construction. 5½ x 6½″. Collection the artist. Photograph: William Gullette

opposite below: Arline Fisch. *Two Squares and ZigZag.* Brooch. 1988. 18-karat gold, hematite. Plaited construction. 1 x 5 x 1″. Collection the artist. Photograph: William Gullette

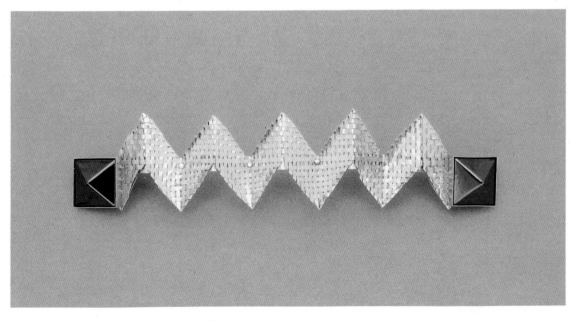

Donald Friedlich

Among his sources of inspiration, Donald Friedlich lists the painter Richard Diebenkorn and the sculptor Isamu Noguchi. In his own aesthetic, Friedlich combines the best of these two artists, uniting colorful abstract composition and irregularly carved stone.

Friedlich enlists a wide range of semiprecious and mundane materials for his formal explorations, including slate, onyx, lapis, gold, and glass. His approach to these materials is sensitive and experimental. Instead of setting stones in a metal base, as is traditional, Freidlich reverses the priority and sets small metal pieces in a larger field of stone.

Friedlich prefers the rectangular or square brooch format, which he tackles like a canvas, setting up compositional dynamics within the frame. Sometimes he engages in a painterly play of color and surface, other times he creates the gradation and texture of small relief sculptures.

In all of his work, Friedlich focuses on the issues of tension and balance. In his three recent series—Interference, Erosion, and Patterns—Friedlich has set up expectations that are then disrupted. Interference creates tension in its interruption of strict geometric forms; Erosion contrasts matte and gloss, sandblasted and polished surfaces to suggest the play of natural and manmade forces on the landscape; Patterns sets up a grid or pattern and then cuts it short. Exploiting the power of irregularity that the Japanese understand so well, Friedlich proves himself to be a master of subtle tension.

above: Donald Friedlich. *Erosion Series Brooch.* 1984. Slate, 18-karat gold, sterling silver. Carved, sandblasted, roller-printed, riveted. 1⅝ x 1⅞ x ⅜". Collection Vanessa Lynn, New York. Photograph: James Beards

opposite: Donald Friedlich. *Pattern Series Brooch.* 1990. Glass, niobium, 18-karat gold, sterling silver. Carved, sandblasted, fabricated, anodized, roller-printed. Collection Seta Nazarian Albrecht, Haworth, N.J. Photograph: James Beards

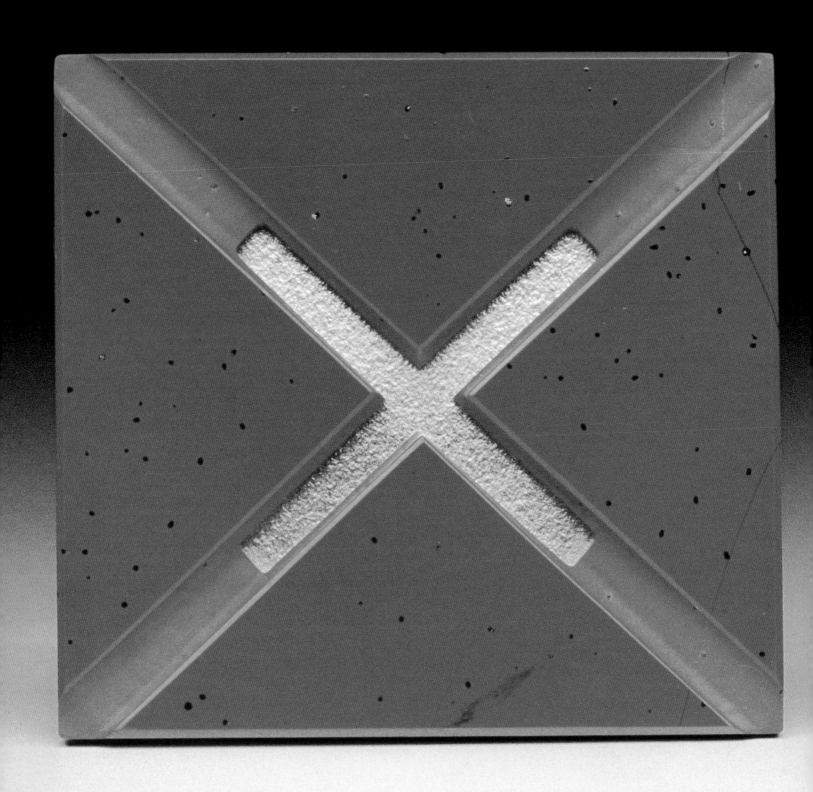

opposite: Donald Friedlich. *Erosion Series Brooch.* 1990. Red jasper, 18-karat gold, sterling silver. Carved, sandblasted, roller-printed, fabricated. 1⁷/₈ x 2¹/₈ x ³/₈″. Collection the artist. Photograph: James Beards

above: Donald Friedlich. *Fragment Series Brooch.* 1991. Brazilian slate, sterling silver. Carved, fabricated, riveted. 1⁷/₈ x 3³/₄ x ³/₈″. Private collection. Photograph: James Beards

Thomas Gentille

"Beauty is a quality I am always seeking," claims Thomas Gentille, and his work bears testament to this guiding consideration. It is rare to find an artist today in any field who commits himself to the pursuit of perfection, and Gentille is one of the few in contemporary jewelry to set this as a goal.

Gentille succeeds by remaining keenly attentive to every formal element in the work. He merges the concerns of the painter, sculptor, and craftsman, keeping an eye on the quality of light and spatial dynamics. It is evident that a great deal of time and concentration are invested in his pieces; one can sense a controlling intellect behind the work.

While Gentille occasionally uses precious materials, they are not the source of his work's value and exquisiteness. Rather, these derive from the beauty he cultivates in the work. According to Gentille, "The less precious the material, the more difficult it is to make it work, to make it speak, to find its soul." However, whether the material is eggshell or ebony, Gentille repeatedly succeeds in making matter speak and finding its soul.

Gentille's work is satisfying in many respects. It provides pleasure in part through the meticulous execution and subtle material effects. It also pleases through quiet surprises and gentle transitions.

left: Thomas Gentille. Pin. 1991. Surell, pure pigment inlay, eggshell. Diam. 4 x ½". Private collection. Photograph: Karen Bell

opposite: Thomas Gentille. *Légion d'Honneur.* Armlet. 1987. ColorCore, metal. Diam. 6¼ x ½". Collection Victoria & Albert Museum, London. Photograph: Courtesy Victoria & Albert Museum

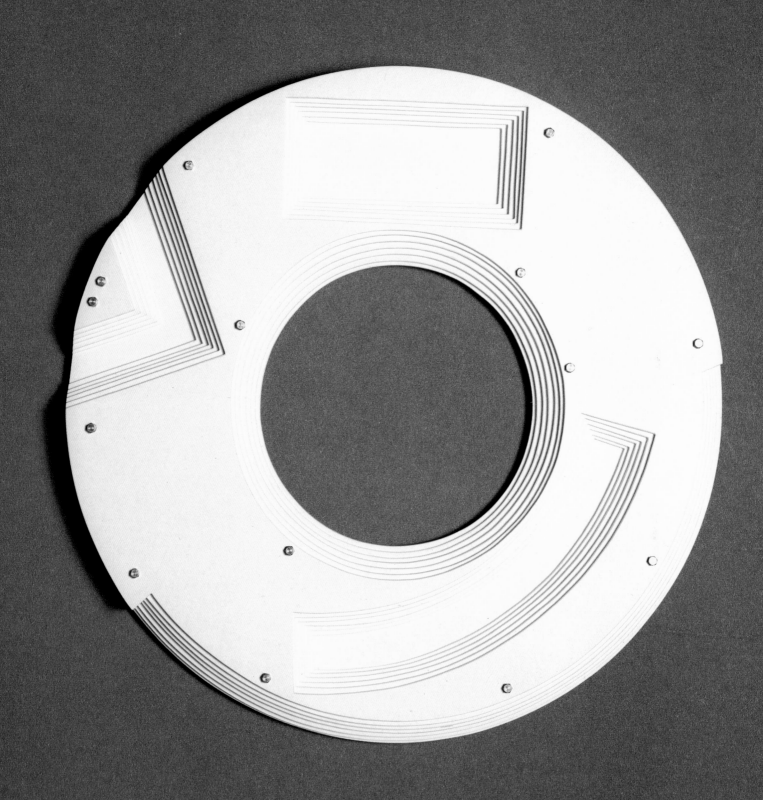

opposite: Thomas Gentille. *Britannia.* Armlet. 1987. Eggshell. 5¾ x 5½″. Photograph: James Arnosky

right: Thomas Gentille. *Shadow of an Armlet from the Fourth Dimension, First Version.* Armlet. 1988. Bronze, anodized aluminum, black industrial paint, Color-Core, acrylic, canvas. Diam. 6½ x ⅛″. Photograph: Karen Bell

below: Thomas Gentille. *Black Form.* Armlet. 1991. Ebony. Diam. 5 x 1½″. Photograph: Karen Bell

Lisa Gralnick

Black is the color one associates with Lisa Gralnick's work, and machinery is the form it most resembles. Black can signify many different things—elegance, mourning, a void—but it cannot be called an inviting color. Though it absorbs light, it refuses to please the eye. Black is a serious color, never frivolous, gay, or charming.

This lack of brightness and visual delight runs counter to the expected qualities of traditional jewelry. Gralnick's jewelry is severe, and it is through such severity, rather than delightfulness, that it commands our attention.

This darkness of tone is combined with machinelike industrial forms. Gralnick's works from the 1980s were primarily constructed from black acrylic sheets, meticulously wrought into tight hollow shapes, with a sleek polish and demeanor. Many allude to the threat of technology, depicting missiles, submarines, and weapons. Others resemble fittings from a tool-and-die shop. All serve as dark artifacts from our industrial culture, at once celebrating and mourning the products of technology.

The work from the 1990s, while still engaged with mechanical forms, suggests the more positive aspect of technology. *Anti-Gravity Neckpiece #5* of 1992, a metal disk with pulley, points to machinery's potential to provide relief. The use of metal, rather than black acrylic, also lightens the visual load of these works.

Whether dark or light, Gralnick's work engages us in a serious dialogue with our manufactured culture. Her work is less about the relationship of the work to the wearer than it is about the wearer's relationship to industrial culture.

left: Lisa Gralnick. Brooch. 1989. Black acrylic, gold. Hollow construction. Diam. 4 x ¼". Private collection. Photograph: George Erml

opposite above: Lisa Gralnick. Three bracelets. 1988. Black acrylic, gold. Hollow construction. Left to right, 3 x 3½ x 3½"; 4½ x 3½ x 3"; 3½ x 3½ x 3½". Private collection; Collection Stedelijk Museum, Amsterdam; Private collection. Photograph: George Erml

opposite below: Lisa Gralnick. Brooch. 1990. 18-karat gold. Fabricated. 1⅛ x 2 x ⅜". Photograph: Ralph Gabriner

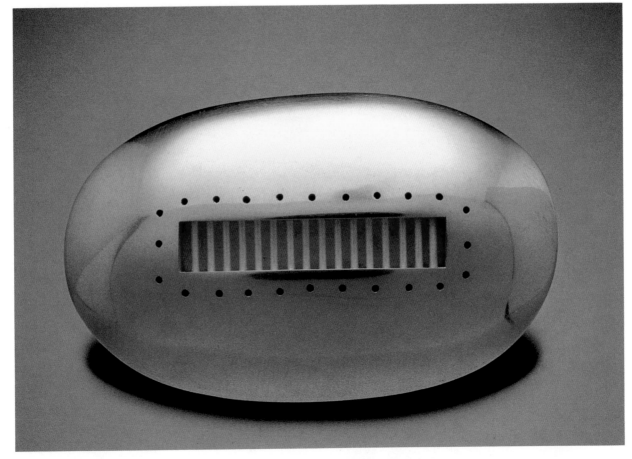

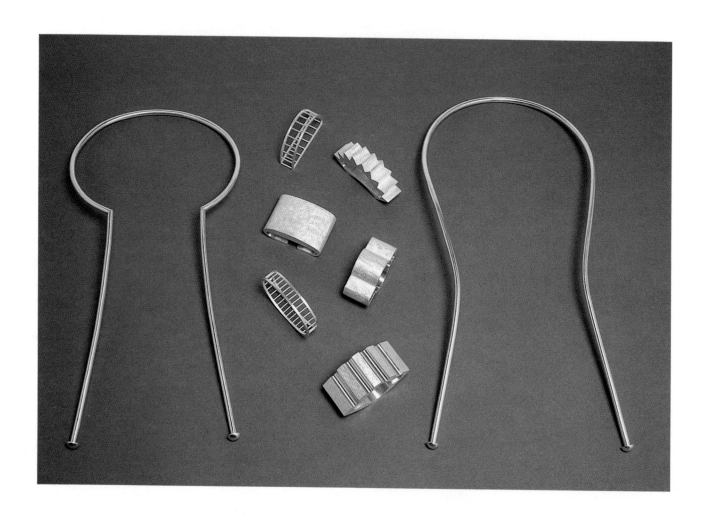

above: Lisa Gralnick. Two neck pieces with attachable forms. 1991. Sterling silver. Fabricated. Neck piece 14 x 6 x ¼", forms approx. 1¼ x 2¼ x ¾". Private collections. Photograph: Bobby Hansson

opposite: Lisa Gralnick. *Anti-gravity Neck-piece #5.* 1992. Sterling silver, 14-karat gold. Fabricated. Chain length 16", pendant and chain 10 x 2 x 1", unwinding to 5'. Private collection. Photograph: Bobby Hansson

Laurie Hall

Laurie Hall could be called the cultural reporter of contemporary jewelry. She is concerned with capturing the world around her, particularly the world of American culture. As Hall says, "I am especially drawn toward depicting the spirit of America." The themes she has addressed include sports, civil rights protest, and the imagery of native Americans.

Her treatment of these subjects is not straight reportage, however; she strongly editorializes her subjects, usually with an eye toward humor. Her work *K.O.* (meaning knockout) features two antique boxing figures with their dukes up. For Hall, "the idea that someone would be wearing a whole boxing match on her chest is funny."

Humor and exuberance are trademarks of Hall's work, to the extent that they sometimes interfere with function. She has made a series of narrative eyeglass frames—one in the shape of a bicycle—that obstruct rather than aid vision. This work was aptly entitled *How Far Will You Go?*, a question one would like to ask Hall herself. She has also done a series of gauntlets with questionable use value but undeniable humor. One pair, entitled *Arms Control,* sports miniature guns and red bull's-eyes.

Hall has said, "I want people to wear rooms." Her jewelry embodies a healthy appetite that craves to include all the colorful stories and strains in our culture.

left: Laurie Hall. *E.A.T. @ McDonalds.* Pin (shoulder location). 1988. Sterling silver, Plexiglas, brass, copper. Fabricated. 3 x 3 x 1½". Private collection. Photograph: Richard Nicol

opposite: Laurie Hall. *Cubist Café.* Necklace. 1987. Oxidized sterling silver. Fabricated. 12 x 8 x ¼". Collection Mia McEldowney, Seattle. Photograph: Roger Schreiber

overleaf left: Laurie Hall. *K.O.* Necklace. 1985. Antique folk figures, brass, copper, leather, charm. Fabricated. 16 x 6 x ½". Collection Sandy Grotta, New Vernon, N.J. Photograph: Tom Grotta

overleaf right: Laurie Hall. *One in Ten.* Necklace. 1989. Sterling silver, bronze, antique game piece. Fabricated. 12 x 6 x ¼". Collection Sandy Grotta, New Vernon, N.J. Photograph: Richard Nicol

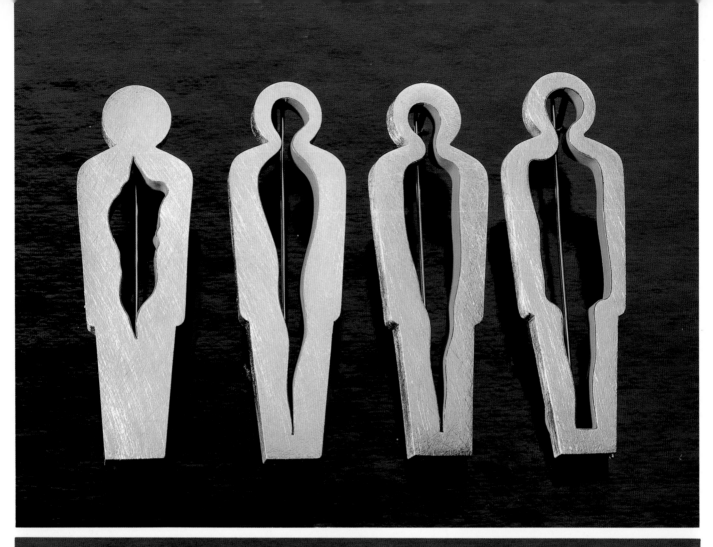

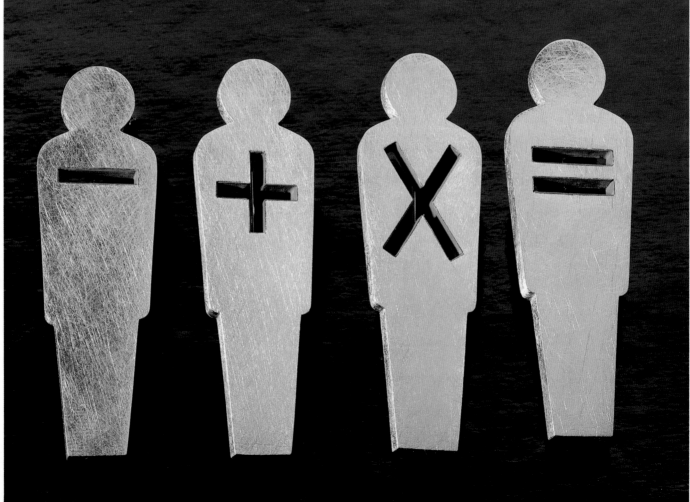

Susan H. Hamlet

Though she is relatively young, Susan Hamlet has in her metalsmith career already spanned the range from complex abstraction to narrative figuration and from jewelry to hollowware vessels. From 1980 to 1987 the artist explored the formal and mechanical properties of metal and spring wire with her Flexible Columns and Shim Bracelets. She continued to exploit the reflectivity and malleability of metal in the succeeding years with her hollowware vessels, which both collected and dispersed light.

Hamlet's past concerns have resurfaced in her recent works of figures in silhouette, *Four Seasons* and *Basic Math*. These latest works reveal a blend of abstraction and figuration, flashy surface effects and narrative symbolism, interior and exterior articulation. In *Four Seasons,* the figure's exterior contour remains intact while its interior contour undergoes an evolution, first taking the shape of a small "fissure" to represent Fall and ending as that of a young woman in Summer. *Basic Math* also presents a fourfold schematization, with each figure bearing a mathematical symbol, like an ironic stigma. The series format allows Hamlet to develop a theme or narrative, and her multiple-part works give the wearers the opportunity to arrange the "characters" on their body, to either reinforce or deny the artist's intended narrative or "equation."

Instead of falling into a multipartite format, Hamlet's recent work conflates the narrative elements into a single work. Forms and symbols are arranged together like still lifes, creating poetic associations rather than narrative story lines.

opposite above: Susan H. Hamlet. *Four Seasons: Fall, Winter, Spring, Summer.* Set of four brooches. 1990. 14-karat gold, lead. Fabricated. Each 2½ x ¾ x ³⁄₁₆″. Collection the artist. Photograph: Tim Sylvia

opposite below: Susan H. Hamlet. *Basic Math.* Set of four brooches. 1990. 14-karat gold, lead. Fabricated. Each 2½ x ¾ x ³⁄₁₆″. Collection the artist. Photograph: Tim Sylvia

right: Susan H. Hamlet. *The Inheritance II.* Brooch. 1993. 14-karat gold. Fabricated. 2 x 1⅛ x ³⁄₈″. Collection the artist. Photograph: Susan H. Hamlet

115

William Harper

William Harper is an artist who has it both ways; he doesn't take an either/or approach to jewelry. His work deftly combines male and female, high and low, beauty and ugliness, sacred and profane, abstraction and representation. It is a feat that many artists could not pull off, but Harper repeatedly unites these opposites in his rich, energetic works.

Harper's materials include everything from gold and opals to pig's teeth and beetles. His subject matter can range from migraine headaches to Christian martyrdom. Whatever the material or subject matter, Harper consistently lavishes great attention on his works, creating jewelry that is wonderfully indulgent and extravagant.

Harper's ability to unite opposites is nicely demonstrated in the artist's series of self-portraits from 1989–90. The series is a mixture of both soul-searching and irreverence. He presents us with *Grotesque Self-Portrait of the Artist as the Goddess Kali* and *Grotesque Self-Portrait of the Artist as a Pagan Baby,* then as *Icon* and *Mute Oracle.* The conjunction of opposites is especially pointed in the *Goddess Kali,* which unites male and female energies, and genitals, in one loaded composition.

This series points out both the malleability of the individual persona and the malleability of jewelry. In the process of exploring himself as a creator and citizen, Harper has discovered the most unlikely results in the world of jewelry.

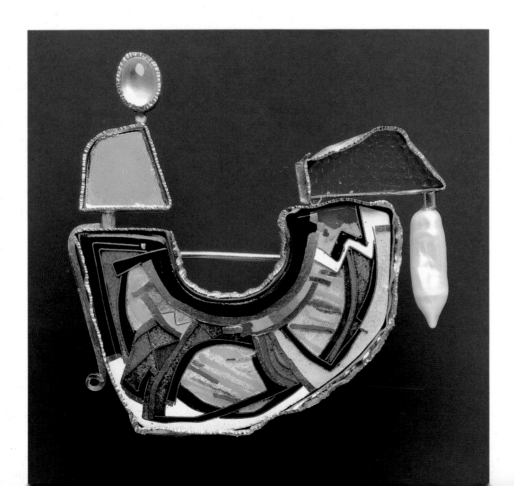

left: William Harper. *The Fake Maharajah.* Brooch. 1986. Gold, cloisonné enamel on fine silver and fine gold, 14- and 24-karat gold, sterling silver, moonstone, pearl, mirror, plastic. Constructed. $2^7/_8$ x $2^{15}/_{16}$ x $2^3/_8$″. Private collection. Photograph: Peter Iverson

opposite: William Harper. *October Fragment.* Brooch. 1991. Gold, cloisonné enamel on fine silver, 14- and 24-karat gold, amethyst, pearl, glass. Constructed. $3^7/_8$ x $2^3/_4$ x $^1/_4$″. Collection Barbara Sue Peay, Cleveland Heights, Ohio. Photograph: Marco Prazzo

overleaf left: William Harper. *Fabergé's Seed.* Brooch. 1992. Gold, cloisonné enamel on fine silver and fine gold, 24- and 14-karat gold, sterling silver, pearls. Constructed. $5^1/_8$ x $2^3/_8$ x $^3/_4$″. Private collection. Photograph: Peter Iverson

overleaf right: William Harper. *The Third Bridal Garden.* Brooch. 1991. Gold, cloisonné enamel on fine silver, 24- and 14-karat gold, sterling silver, pearls, pyrite. Constructed. $3^{15}/_{16}$ x $2^9/_{16}$ x $^5/_8$″. Private collection. Photograph: Peter Iverson

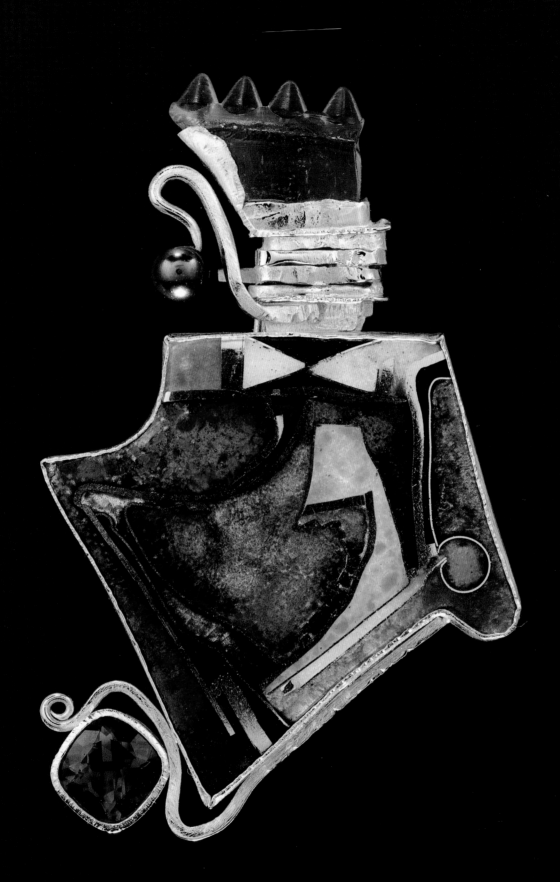

Mary Lee Hu

Though Mary Lee Hu works in the traditional jewelry material of gold and employs a technique dating back centuries, her work represents a distinct approach to contemporary jewelry. After years of experimentation she has developed a highly sophisticated method of weaving metal wires into exquisitely crafted neck pieces, earrings, and bracelets.

Hu began experimenting with woven metal after taking a weaving course in graduate school. She soon applied the lessons from fiber to her metalwork. Hu's work, like textile weaving, displays surface texture and pattern created by the play of shadow and light, negative and positive space. Hu achieves these effects without the use of a loom; instead, she has mastered a process called twining, similar to that used in basketry. But unlike typical basketry or loom weaving, which has a single warp and weft, Hu uses multiple warps and wefts, resulting in her signature double twining technique. This approach allows her to produce engagingly intricate effects.

Though Hu was unaware of earlier precedents when she developed her woven metal jewelry, she has since discovered historical forerunners for her technique. Similar approaches can be found in the ornament of the Middle Ages and in that of the Middle East and Japan. Like the works from these other cultures, Hu's pieces are designed to compliment and adorn the human body.

below: Mary Lee Hu. *Choker #74.* 1988. 18- and 22-karat gold. Twined, fabricated. 8³/₄ x 8¹/₄ x 1¹/₂″. Private collection. Photograph: Richard Nicol

opposite above: Mary Lee Hu. *Choker #75.* 1988. 18- and 22-karat gold. Twined, forged, fabricated. 7 x 6¹/₄ x ³/₄″. Collection the artist. Photograph: Richard Nicol

opposite below: Mary Lee Hu. *Bracelet #37.* 1986. 18- and 22-karat gold, lapis lazuli. Twined, forged, fabricated. 3¹/₄ x 2³/₄ x ¹/₂″. Collection the artist. Photograph: Richard Nicol

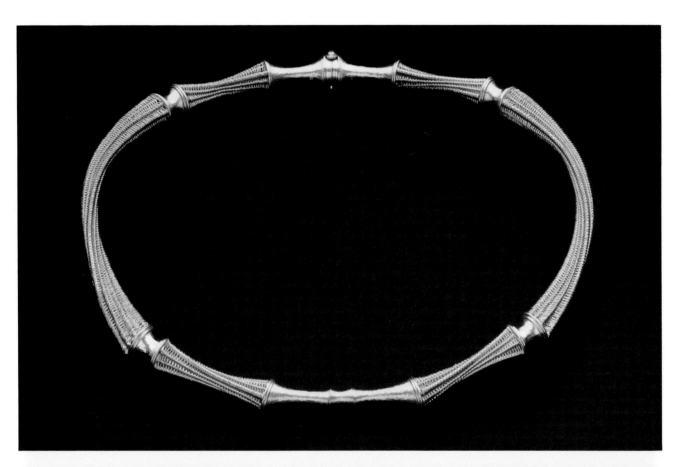

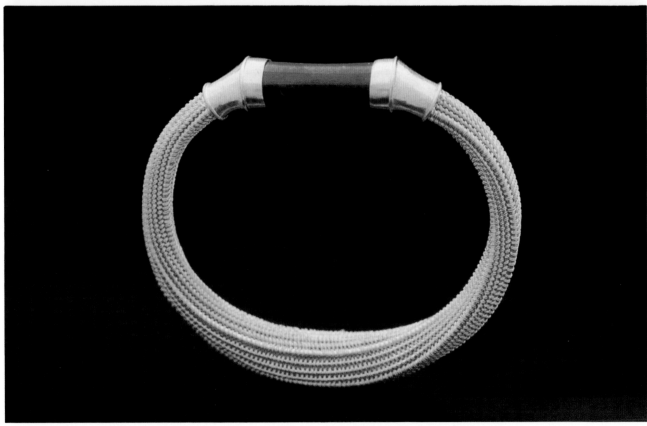

John Iversen

John Iversen's works are materialistic in the best sense of the word: they reveal a respect for materials and let them do the talking. As the artist says, "All my jewelry is about the secret which lies hidden in the materials I use. It wants to be discovered." Such an approach to materials can be seen in an alabaster pin of 1978, thinly carved and laminated to highlight its transparency and marbly gradations.

This indulgent treatment is found foremost in Iversen's use of enamel, which he crafts in order to highlight its distinctive properties. Iversen handles enamel like no other artist, treating it not as surface color but as solid matter to be carved and filed into shape. In Iverson's hands color becomes tangible substance. His bracelets of pebble-shaped enamel parts have the density and richness of real lapis or turquoise.

Years of goldsmithing and jewelry design both in the United States and abroad developed Iverson's innovative and technical strength. The same experimental approach and skill are displayed in his "needlepoint" or basket bracelets, which are constructed in string and then cast in metal.

below: John Iversen. Bracelet. 1988. Turquoise enamel, copper, nickel, gold plate. Enameled, constructed. 3 x 7$\frac{1}{2}$ x $\frac{1}{8}$". Private collection. Photograph: Karen Bell

opposite: John Iversen. Bracelet. 1989. Oxidized bronze. Cast. Diam. 5$\frac{1}{2}$ x 8". Private collection. Photograph: Teresa Misagal, Artwear Catalog Series 1992

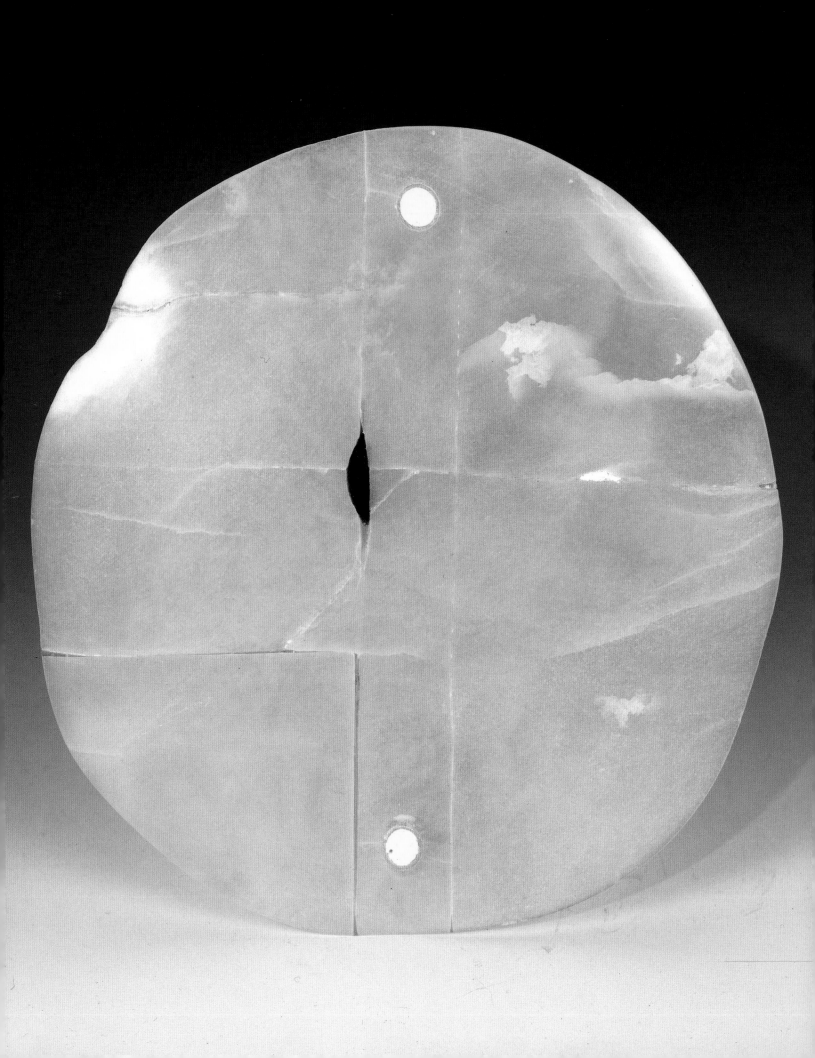

John Iversen. *Tower Bracelets.* 1979. Rusted steel. Folded tension structured. Left to right, 5 x 3 x 3″, 6¹/₂ x 3¹/₂ x 3¹/₂″. Private collection. Photograph: Karen Bell

John Iversen. Pin. 1989. Red and blue enamel, copper, nickel, gold plate. Enameled, constructed. Diam. 5 x ¹/₈″. Private collection. Photograph: Karen Bell

opposite: John Iversen. *Alabaster Pin.* 1978. Alabaster. Carved, laminated. Diam. 5 x ³/₁₆″. Private collection. Photograph: Karen Bell

Daniel Jocz

Daniel Jocz's recent rings are some of the most exuberant and stunning works to be found in contemporary jewelry today. Beginning his career as a sculptor, Jocz worked on constructed bracelets through the 1980s, and since 1988 he began exploring the possibilities of the ring format.

Many of Jocz's rings cannot be worn on the fingers. The artist is more interested in the thought of their wearability; they become more exciting because they seem to have the potential for use. Uncontained by the demands of the wearer, Jocz is free to be extravagant in his creations. And extravagant he is. The finger hole of the "ring" serves more as a base or pedestal for his striking growths and forms. The stark geometry of the base plays off the colorful and exuberant protruding shapes. In some of his pieces, he achieved the pure rich color and crusty texture of the protrusions by using polymer clays.

Jocz's rings deal with the nature of ceremonies and forms of play. His 1991 ring series is even called Forms at Play. Another series, entitled Ceremonies for the City, attempts to convey various civic aspirations and goals, from celebration to work. Jocz continues his explorations in his 1992 Protos series, which pairs essential contrasts, such as geometric and organic, cold metal and rich color, stark geometry and baroque volume. These are truly expressive forms that do not need to be worn to be appreciated for their lively and dynamic energy.

Jocz's newest work, a series of narrative brooches, demonstrates an almost freehand approach, much like drawing in a sketchbook. These brooches are a direct response to a particular place, incident, or vision.

opposite: Daniel Jocz. *Zuc Series.* Ring. 1992. Sterling silver, 14-karat gold. Soldered construction, brushed finish. 1⅝ x 1 x 1″. Photograph: Dean Powell

right: Daniel Jocz. *Iceberg Series.* Ring. 1992. Sterling silver, 14- and 18-karat gold. Soldered construction, brushed finish. 1⅞ x 1⅛ x ¾″. Photograph: Dean Powell

overleaf left: Daniel Jocz. *The Muse Leaves (Ceremonies for the City).* Ring. 1990. Sterling and fine silver, 14-karat gold, nickel. Soldered construction, patina, file-finished. 2½ x 2½ x 2″. Photograph: Dean Powell

overleaf above right: Daniel Jocz. *Proto's Series.* Rings. 1990. Nickel, polymer clay, pigment. Soldered hollow construction. Each 2½ x 1 x ⅜–¾″. Photograph: Dean Powell

overleaf below right: Daniel Jocz. *Sunset Central France—A State of Mind.* From "The Sketch Book" Brooch series. 1993. Sterling silver, acrylic paint. Bent, pierced, soldered, textured, painted. 2 x 2½ x ¼″. Photograph: Dean Powell

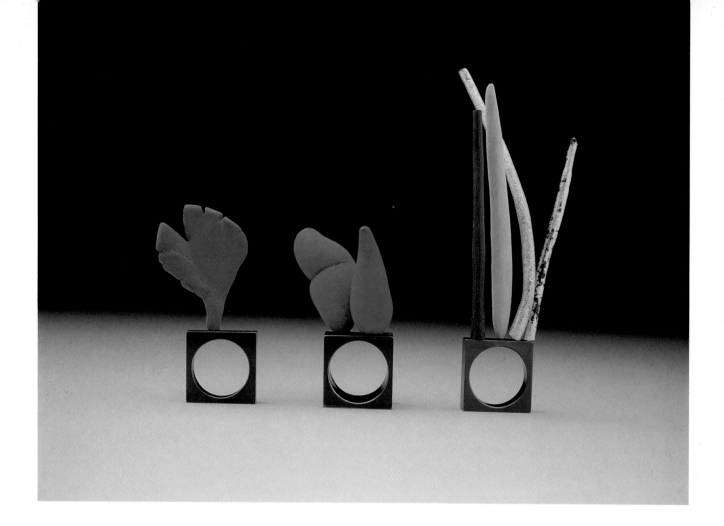

Robin Kranitzky and Kim Overstreet

The duo of Robin Kranitzky and Kim Overstreet exemplifies the narrative tradition in contemporary American jewelry. Like others in this vein, they produce not true narratives but fragments of larger implied story lines. This fragmentation is due partly to the limited confines of the brooch format and partly to their intention of creating mystery through incompletion.

Their ongoing series Lost and Found is a medley of miniature assemblages, rich with association. Among the discarded or "lost" materials that have "found" their way into these works are shells, charms, toys, and finials. These salvaged materials join company with a variety of other mediums, including metal, paint, paper, and colored pencil.

It is not surprising that the artists cite Joseph Cornell and René Magritte as artistic inspirations. Influences of the poetic shadow boxes of the former and the fantastic juxtapositions of the latter can be traced in the jewelers' work. Like the art of the Surrealists, these miniature worlds serve as mental irritants, arousing a process of free association. In the process of beholding them, we alternately lose and find our train of thought.

opposite above left: Robin Kranitzky and Kim Overstreet. *Nothing Left to Chance.* Brooch. 1990. Silver, Micarta, Plexiglas, copper, polymer clay, found objects. Carved, inlaid, assembled, formed, molded. 4 x 2½ x ¾". Private collection, courtesy Hope Palmer. Photograph: Robin Kranitzky

opposite above right: Robin Kranitzky and Kim Overstreet. *Sinking Fast.* Brooch. 1990. Copper, silver, Micarta, Plexiglas, polymer clay, found objects. Carved, inlaid, assembled, formed, molded. 3¾ x 2⅝ x ¾". Private collection, courtesy Helen Drutt Gallery. Photograph: Robin Kranitzky

opposite below: Robin Kranitzky and Kim Overstreet. *The Story Told.* Brooch. 1990. Brass, silver, copper, Plexiglas, polymer clay, found objects. Carved, inlaid, assembled, formed, molded. 4¼ x 2 x ¾". Private collection, courtesy Isabel Allende. Photograph: Robin Kranitzky

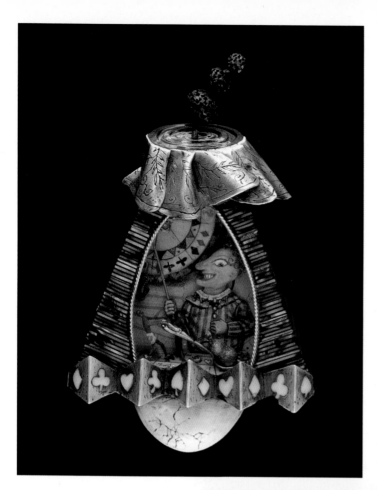

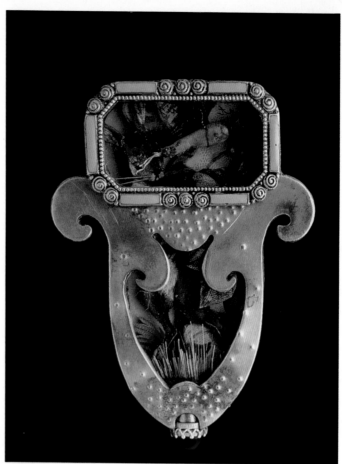

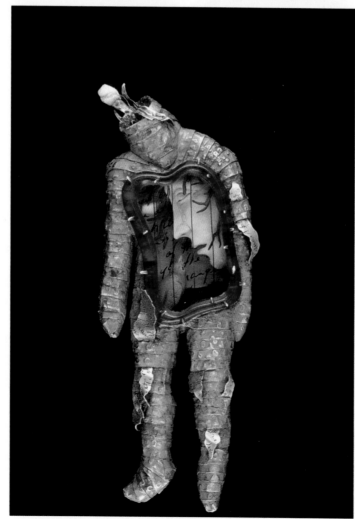

Shana Kroiz

"I choose to celebrate the human form through my work," declares Shana Kroiz. Kroiz achieves this goal by creating forms that evoke the shape and feel of the human body.

This involvement with the human form is clearly expressed in a trio of brooches entitled *Fetal, Childhood,* and *Maturity*; each stage of human development is abstractly rendered through evocative shapes. A similar abstract treatment of the body is found in Kroiz's silhouette brooches that recall the swollen contours of Paleolithic fertility figures.

Though her jewelry often assumes anatomical shapes like spines, thighs, or fleshy folds, Kroiz takes her inspiration from hard tools and weaponry. These tool forms become abstracted and generalized in her work—tamed in the process of formal simplification. They are further tempered by the application of colored enamel.

Through her organic interpretations, instruments of destruction become graceful and mild; geometry is softened into curves. Kroiz's sensually engaging works effectively disarm human technology while simultaneously empowering the wearer through "figure-flattering" forms.

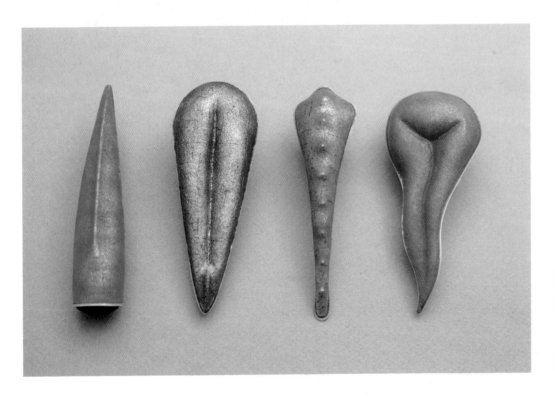

left: Shana Kroiz. *Group.* Brooches. 1993. Copper, enamel, silver, wood. Formed, enameled, carved. 5 x 7 x ¾". Private collection. Photograph: Shana Kroiz

opposite: Shana Kroiz. Necklace. 1992. Copper, enamel, silver, rubber. Carved, electroformed, enameled. 16 x 15 x ½". Photograph: Shana Kroiz

Rebekah Laskin

With their square formats and subtly layered colors and textures, Rebekah Laskin's brooches resemble miniature abstract paintings. Laskin cites as key influences Abstract Expressionist artists such as Robert Motherwell and Helen Frankenthaler, with whom she shares a concern for spatial interplay and surface effects on a two-dimensional surface. Unlike these large-scale "heroic" painters, Laskin explores such compositional dynamics on an intimate scale.

The artist develops her compositions by layering a variety of materials, enamels, and pigments. Some of the layers are later removed or peeled back to reveal the underlying support or a small embedded object. Exploring the multiple levels and partially hidden elements draws the viewer into the piece. Laskin's works are left untitled, encouraging the viewer to enjoy their formal and sensual properties without reference to specific subjects.

Van LeBus

Under the motto "Give me your flotsam and jetsam forever," Van LeBus takes castaway objects and redeems them in assemblage jewelry. As in all assemblage and collage art, LeBus's works offer surprising juxtapositions and unlikely combinations. But LeBus adds an extra ingredient to his exuberant assemblages, namely, a genuine affection for the objects he collects.

This compassion for small, discarded things fuels his life and work. According to LeBus, "There are thousands of little things that cry out for my attention. They say, 'Please don't walk away. Pick me up, keep me. I don't want to go to a landfill to rot away and be forgotten.'" Fortunately for us and for the objects he collects, LeBus gives these things refuge in his wonderful works.

Among the "little things" that LeBus has saved are a fishing cork, a baby shoe, a rearview mirror, piano keys, tennis racket strings, rattlesnake tails, forks, razor blades, fingernails, and armadillo vertebrae. Looking at LeBus's work is like foraging in a flea market or curiosity shop; you cannot predict what you will find or in what combination.

Even LeBus's tools share in this serendipity. Many of them were found at flea markets, and they include an old ice pick, a doorknob axle, surgical tongs, fingernail clippers, razor blades, and steak knives. Aside from the sheer joy LeBus's works provide, they also remind us that beauty is not only in the eye of the beholder but that everything looks wonderful through an affectionate eye.

Van LeBus. *Does the Moon Cry?* Pin. 1988. Yellow pencil slice, fingernail, iridescent bug leg, pincushion cactus thorn, mouse tooth, bird-point arrowhead, aluminum zipper tooth, watch gear slice and hands, dictating plastic disk, air hose, 1950s tennis racket string, antique lady's watch face with hand-painted numbers, cross section of weather stripping, razor-blade shard. Assembled, laminated. Diam. 2 x ³/₈". Collection Larry Millar. Photograph: Steve Butman

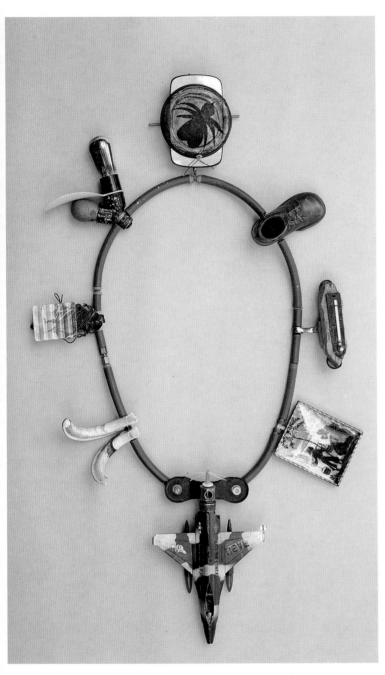

Van LeBus. *Super Hero.* Neck piece. 1990. Toy jet mounted on iron and brass water sprinkler; photograph in steel frame; mercury thermometer mounted on wood with bottlecaps; electroplated baby shoe; rubber fly and rearview mirror; fishing cork, television tube, and shoehorn mounted in double light socket; fiberglass, leather, wire, and old harness buckles; boar tusks; filling station air hose; plumbing washers. Fabricated, assembled. 46 x 22 x 4″. Collection the artist. Photograph: Steve Butman

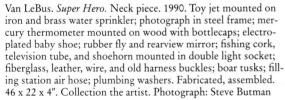

Van LeBus. *Billiard, Ballet, Café.* Neck piece. 1981. Fishing lures, antique ivory cue ball, petrified shark tooth, nutmeg grater, schoolroom globe time zone disk, vintage laminate, old ivory piano keys (used as links, softened with vinegar solution and sewn with fishing line), other found objects. Fabricated, assembled. 28 x 16 x 2½″. Collection the artist. Photograph: Steve Butman

Leslie Leupp

opposite: Leslie Leupp. *Bracelet #NY387* (with stand). 1987. Anodized aluminum. Fabricated. 3½ x 6″. Photograph: Robert Suddarth

below: Leslie Leupp. *Three Bracelets: Solidified Reality, Frivolous Vitality, Compound Simplicity.* 1984. Steel, plastic, linoleum, laminate, aluminum. Constructed. Each 3 x 4 x 3″. Private collections. Photograph: Leslie Leupp

"Objects empower people," says Leslie Leupp. Accordingly, he produces dramatic objects that live up to this tenet, granting the wearer power of choice and participation. Elaborately rigged and physically involving, Leupp's works transform the wearer into a user, increasing their active role in the artistic relationship.

Leupp enlists the most unusual materials and construction techniques to produce these involving works. Wielding such nontraditional materials as linoleum, Formica, vinyl, knitting needles, coils, and twigs with great skill, he explores the possibilities of suspension and tension, both within the piece and upon the wearer's body.

The dynamic tension that Leupp strives to create is tied to his view of the body as an active object experienced in the round. Whereas much jewelry is conceived as two-dimensional, resting on the body as a flat plane, Leupp aims to add projective forms and assertive new angles to the human body. His brooches, for example, are designed to be propped on the neck and shoulder.

All of these engineering and sculptural effects are geared to Leupp's overall goal of wearer responsibility. "I want you to be disturbed," says Leupp. "I want some mental and physical discomfort, a mental awareness, a commitment."

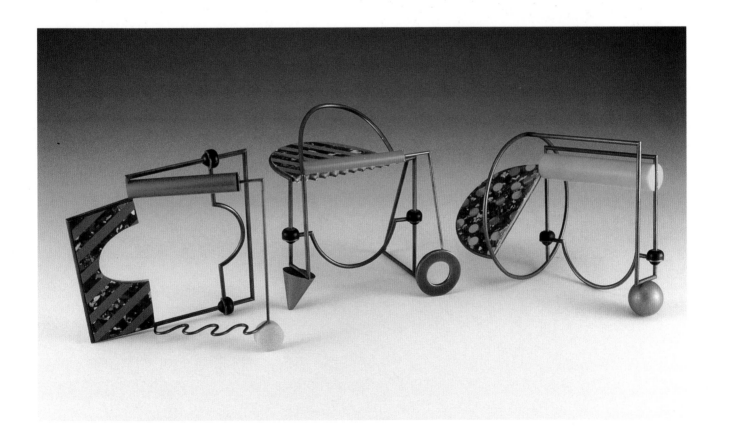

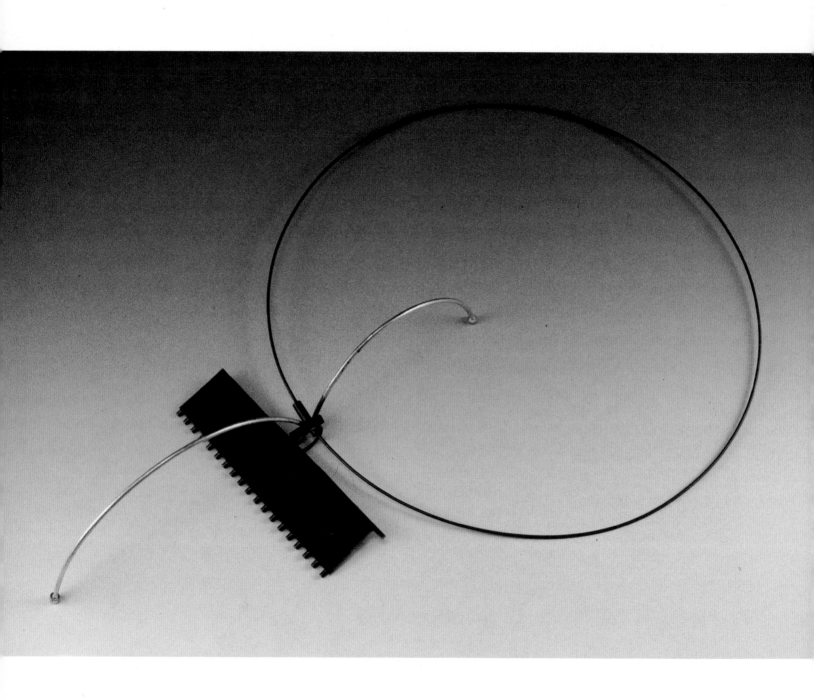

Thomas Mann

Thomas Mann, who describes his work as "theatrical," has carried his early experience as a stage set designer into the miniaturized world of jewelry, creating drama by juggling a wide range of forms and materials. His assemblages juxtapose old and new, hard and soft, threat and seduction in complex scenarios. The script is always open-ended, as his messages are conveyed in an indirect manner.

Much of Mann's work falls under the heading of "Techno Romantic," a term he uses for his production-line jewelry. These works, which usually feature a heart rendered in high-tech hardware, are attempts to humanize technology. Instead of hearts of gold, he gives us hearts of steel and aluminum, lending emotional overtones to otherwise inorganic materials.

Mann also uses his formidable powers to address issues other than romance. He has done a series on world hunger (Food for Thought) and on environmental threats (Endangered Species). These works often include photographs or postcards—which he also used in his self-portrait series—to multiply the meanings and associations possible.

Mann has ventured from jewelry's wearable scale to produce wall-hung works as well. The viewers figure prominently in these works, many of which incorporate mirrors, completing the sculpture with their reflection. Whether his creations perform on a wall or a body, Mann's intent remains the same: to engage us in a dramatic encounter.

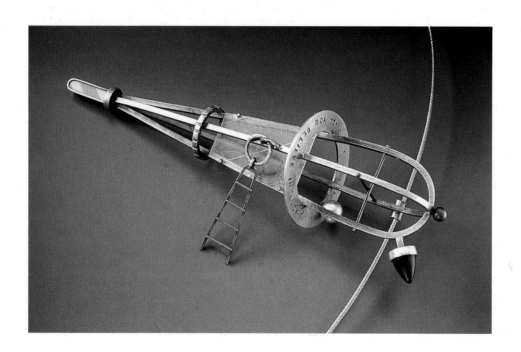

left: Thomas Mann. *Space Frame Neck Piece (Do You Believe in Luck?)*. 1992. Silver, bronze, aluminum, steel, laminated acrylic resin, fiberglass. Fabricated, constructed. 6 x 1¼ x 1¼". Private collection. Photograph: Will Crocker

opposite: Thomas Mann. *Da Da Diva.* Brooch. 1990. Aluminum, bronze, acrylic resin, silver, paper. Fabricated, constructed. 4 x 2½". Photograph: Will Crocker

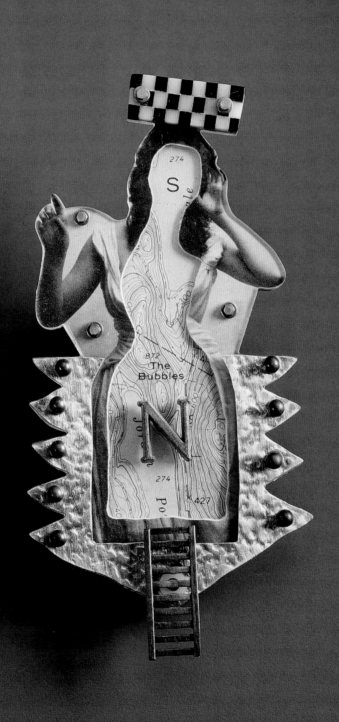

Richard Mawdsley

Richard Mawdsley's jewelry is fantastic in the best sense of the term. He forges in metal fantasy worlds of his own invention. Mawdsley's imagination is matched by his technical virtuosity, and he has produced some of the most striking tour de forces in contemporary jewelry.

Mawdsley's early *Feast Bracelet* of 1974 provides an ideal example of his mastery. It is literally a feast for the eyes, offering a complete dining spread, including miniature fruit, cutlery, and vessels. Mawdsley can translate this craftmanship into real scale and has made functional drinking chalices.

Just as Mawdsley's work shifts scale, it is not marked by any one style. While his overall aesthetic could be called Mannerist or Baroque, many of his works mix sinuous Art Nouveau curves with Art Deco streamlining. His preferred material, metal tubing, brings with it machinelike qualities, while the precious stones and human imagery suggest more organic life.

His subject matter is equally eclectic, often centered around a female figure. He has done everything from a *Medusa* to *Goneril, Regan, Cordelia,* to *Wonder Woman in Her Bicentennial Finery*—ranging from ancient Greek mythology to Shakespeare's *King Lear* to contemporary popular culture. It is to Mawdsley's credit that he can harness all these sources in his elaborate compositions.

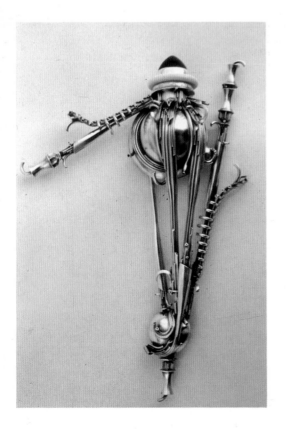

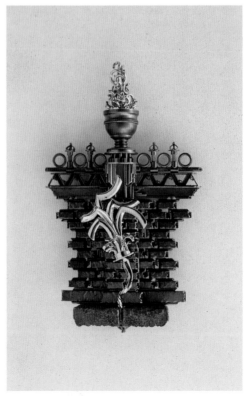

left: Richard Mawdsley. *Oculi Rectus Superiorus #2.* Pin. 1982. Sterling silver, ivory, black onyx. Fabricated. 4½ x 3 x ¾". Private collection. Photograph: Richard Mawdsley

right: Richard Mawdsley. *Garden Wall.* Pin. 1991. Sterling silver, gold plate. Fabricated. 3¾ x 2¾ x ½". Photograph: Richard Mawdsley

opposite: Richard Mawdsley. *Corsage #2.* Pin. 1989. 18-karat gold, sterling silver, pearls, enamel on copper (by Bill Helwig). Fabricated. 7 x 4 x 1¼". Photograph: Duane Powell

Bruce Metcalf

Bruce Metcalf makes intense little vignettes that one can wear on one's breast the same way others wear their hearts on their sleeves. His cartoonlike works feature characters engaged in scenes of angst or frustration. These agitated scenes at first seem sincere, fueled by real emotional strain, but they ultimately reveal themselves as humorous or dry statements about human foibles and anxieties. Metcalf refers to the works as displaying "ironic negativity," a kind of double negative that ends up cancelling out the original emotional problem.

A case in point is the piece *Blind and Stupid in Paradise,* which features a figure whose torso has turned into a cactus and who has a pillow bound to his face, blinding him to his tropical landscape backdrop. Rather then elicit compassion, this suffering figure elicits a nod of dismay at human weakness and insensitivity. Similarly, *Headlock* offers a visual pun illustrating the condition of being hopelessly trapped in one's own head.

Determined not to have his jewelry just sit there "looking pretty," Metcalf uses exaggerated and expressionistic forms for critical and humanistic ends. His zany and energetic depictions, though small, pack a large wallop.

below left: Bruce Metcalf. *Learning to Build.* Pin. 1989. Silver, wood, copper. Fabricated, cast. 4 x 3½ x 1″. Collection Lizzy Yoo, Seoul. Photograph: Bruce Metcalf

below right: Bruce Metcalf. *Headful of Bad Ideas.* Pin. 1989. Sterling silver. Fabricated, cast. 5 x 4″. Collection Mark Del Vecchio, New York. Photograph: Bruce Metcalf

opposite: Bruce Metcalf. *Wood Pin #32.* 1988. Maple, ivory, brass, 23-karat gold leaf over paint. Fabricated, carved. 5 x 3¾″. Collection Gail Brown, Wynnewood, Pa. Photograph: Bruce Metcalf

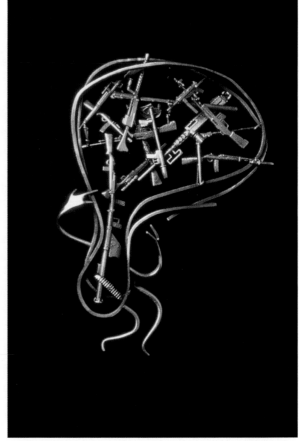

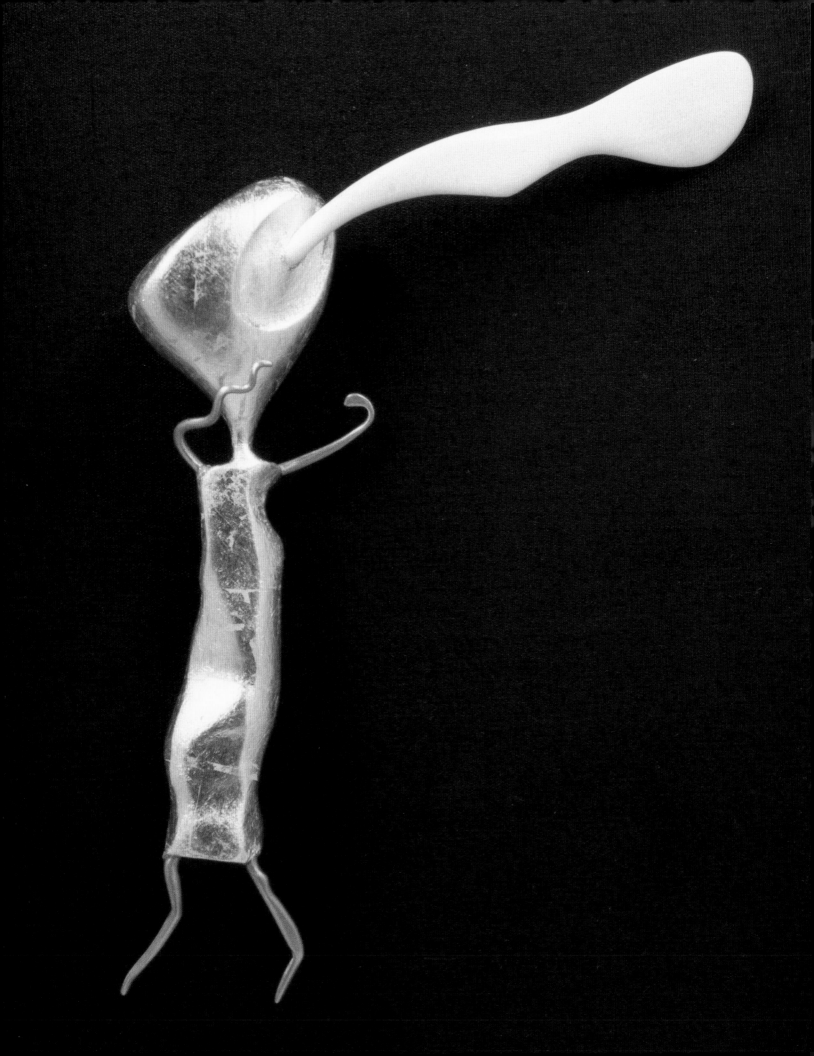

Myra Mimlitsch-Gray

While Marilyn Monroe sang "Diamonds Are a Girl's Best Friend," Myra Mimlitsch-Gray asserts the less benign, more unfriendly aspects of this crystalline carbon, producing a highly critical form of wearable art. Typically a source of status and prestige, the diamond under Mimlitsch-Gray's hands assumes an abrasive and threatening character.

These sinister implications of the diamond are demonstrated in her Timepiece series. The notion of time is implied both by the works' round contours, which suggest the face of a clock, and by the pendulumlike bars protruding from the center. Beyond merely illustrating the shape of time, these works actually mark the passage of time through the motion of the diamond-tipped pendulum, which scratches the glass lens beneath. The diamond is recast as an agent of destruction, a material that destroys less powerful substances.

For those who wish to pursue the idea, Mimlitsch-Gray's works make a rather profound, albeit silent, philosophical point. They argue that the identity or value of a material rests in its function or use, not in its essence or being. Mimlitsch-Gray is one of a few contemporary jewelers who put forth such conceptual reevaluations of materials. The wearer of her works becomes the unwitting carrier of this radical message.

opposite above left: Myra Mimlitsch-Gray. *Timepiece.* Kinetic brooch. 1987. Silver, stainless steel, lens, cubic zirconia. Fabricated. 3 x 2 x ¼". Collection Rachelle Thiewes, El Paso. Photograph: Tom Brummett

opposite above right: Myra Mimlitsch-Gray. *Timepiece.* Kinetic brooch. 1988. 14-karat gold, lens, diamonds, abrasive disk. Fabricated. 2¼ x 1½ x ¼". Collection the artist. Photograph: Myra Mimlitsch-Gray

opposite below: Myra Mimlitsch-Gray. Ring. 1993. 24-karat gold over brass, brass charms. Fabricated. 4 x 4 x 2". Photograph: Myra Mimlitsch-Gray

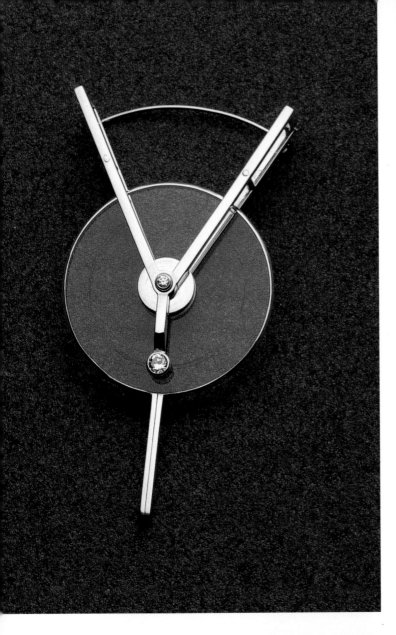

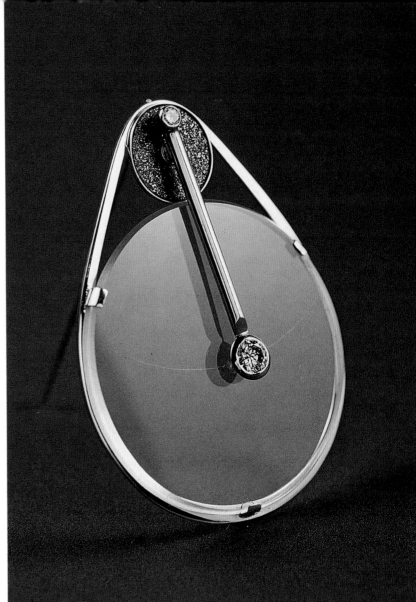

Valerie Mitchell

Valerie Mitchell's work reveals a clear love of materials and formal processes. This enjoyment is expressed both in the type of materials chosen and in the range of surface effects and textures, from rich crusty patinas to velvety finishes to scratchy cross-hatchings. Her facility with materials is demonstrated in her deft handling of lightweight cement, a most unruly and disagreeable substance.

The textural contrasts of hard and soft, rough and smooth also show up in the shapes that Mitchell explores. Her earlier works were based on the products of industry, echoing industrial forms like bridges, machines, and tools. More recently she has turned her attention to nature's designs and engineering, creating organic structures resembling pods, mollusks, and protozoa.

Though Mitchell has alternated between the manmade and the organic, she does not see a need to choose between nature and culture, the "raw and the cooked." The artist explains, "I am interested in the harmony between what nature provides and what we implement (ornament)." Indeed, her finely wrought wearable objects accord perfectly with the human form. Many works, like *Raft,* are made to rest lightly on the shoulder, perched in the crook of the neck like a docked boat. Mitchell's jewelry is adornment in the best sense of the word; it dresses up and flatters the body—nature's creation—with human artifice.

left: Valerie Mitchell. *Raft.* Brooch. 1988. Copper, 10-karat gold. Electroformed copper, patina. 5 x 2½ x 2″. Photograph: Mark Stephenson

opposite: Valerie Mitchell. *Conduit.* Pendant. 1992. Copper. Electroformed, patina. 1½ x 5½″. Private collection, Washington, D.C. Photograph: Mark Johann

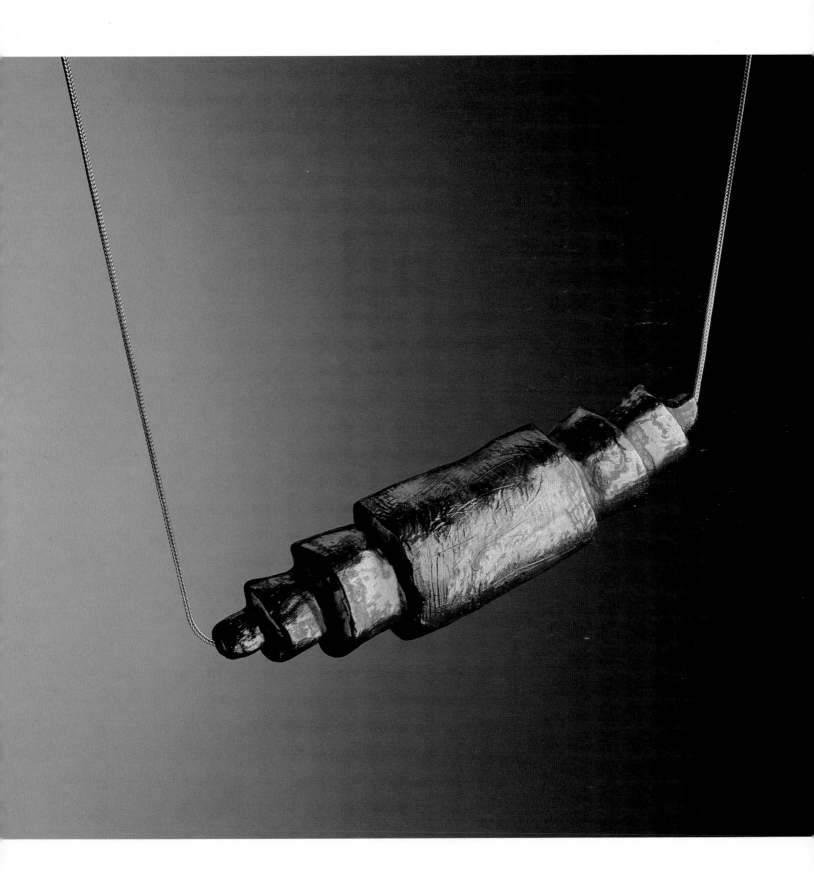

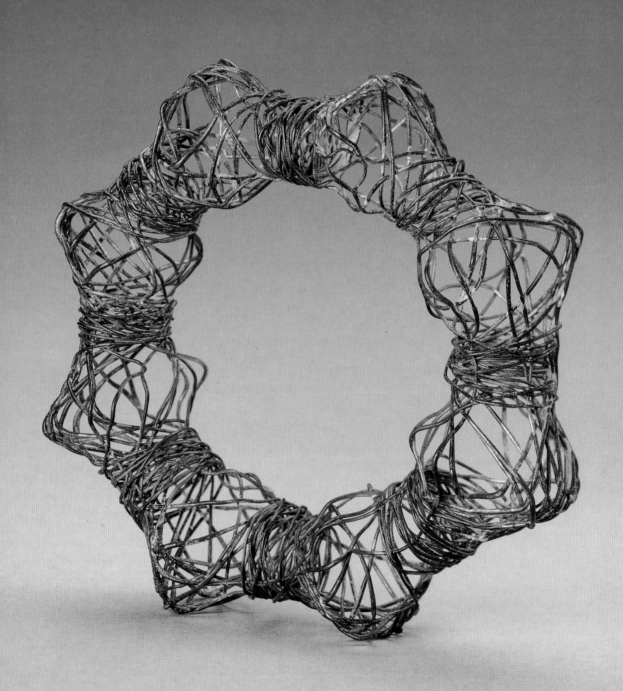

above: Valerie Mitchell. *Vortex* and *Boat.*
Two brooches. 1989. Sterling silver,
bronze, cement. Constructed, fabricated,
file-finished. Right, 6 x 1½ x 1″. Photograph: Marc Bernier

opposite: Valerie Mitchell. *Wire Armature.*
Bracelet. 1991. Copper wire. Constructed,
patina. 4 x 4 x 1″. Private collection. Photograph: Mark Johann

155

Eleanor Moty

Though Eleanor Moty began her jewelry career experimenting widely with electroforming and photoetching techniques, since the late 1970s she has focused her attention on the graphic potential of natural crystals. The artist is drawn to these semiprecious stones not for their intrinsic or market value, nor for their presumed mystical powers, but rather for their strong aesthetic properties.

The specific type of stone that Moty favors—rutilated and tourmalinated quartz—is characteristically marked by rodlike spears of the mineral rutile. These dark mineral rods, frozen within the transparent stone, form strong linear configurations. The artist has made it her task to locate and reinforce these abstract compositions lodged within the stone.

Moty employs many compositional devices to underline the graphic dynamic within the natural material. Sometimes the metal frame of the brooch echoes the geometric structure of the rutile rods, taking the shape of a triangle or other polygon. The directional flow of the stone is further emphasized by smaller metal elements applied to the frame. The cut and polish of the stone are also carefully calculated to enhance the play of line within the quartz. In this way setting, cut, and polish all serve to reinforce the lapidary design; artifice is placed in the service of nature.

Though Moty has restricted both the material and format in her recent jewelry—working exclusively with the brooch format—there are still enough variables in her work to insure its liveliness. The one-of-a-kind quartz, with its irregularities and unique structure, always remains subject to its environment when it is worn, changing character in response to the wearer's clothing and the light that strikes it.

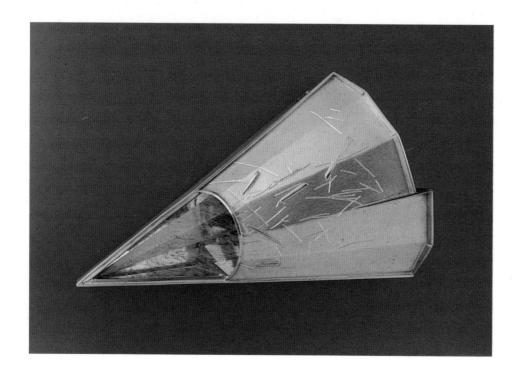

left: Eleanor Moty. *Conical Brooch.* 1989. Sterling silver, 14-karat gold, rutilated quartz. Fabricated. 2¼ x 3¾ x ⅞". Photograph: Eleanor Moty

opposite: Eleanor Moty. *Icicle Brooch.* 1987. Sterling silver, 18-karat gold, rutilated quartz. Fabricated. 5⅝ x 1 x ¾". Collection Robert Pfannebecker. Photograph: Bill Fritsch

left: Eleanor Moty. *Interrupted Vertical.*
Brooch. 1990. Sterling silver, 22- and 18-
karat gold, rutilated quartz, topaz. Fabricated. 4 x 1⅜ x ½″. Collection the artist.
Photograph: Bill Fritsch

opposite: Eleanor Moty. *Phantom Brooch.*
1988. Sterling silver, 18-karat gold, phantom quartz, black paper Micarta. Fabricated. 2¾ x 2⅛ x ½″. Private collection.
Photograph: Eleanor Moty

Ted Muehling

It is a maxim that there are no right angles in nature. Ted Muehling's sensuously organic work—some of the most curvaceously pleasing jewelry on the contemporary scene—is in keeping with this maxim. His forms contain no sharp angles or corners, just variations on swelling round shapes.

Not surprisingly, nature serves Muehling as a constant guide for his aesthetic; he surrounds himself with organic treasures like shells, eggs, fossils, and insects. Rather than recreate nature's forms, he uses the vocabulary of the natural world to create his own generalized interpretation of nature. Although not one of a kind, each piece Muehling makes is handwrought.

The resulting works have the organic character of shells, seeds, and pods but add the sophistication and polish of fine craftsmanship. His earrings dangle from the earlobes like fruits, while his brooches cling to the body like insects or seed pods. These gently swelling ornaments mesh perfectly with the female form, echoing a woman's natural curves. Muehling's satisfying organicity brings to mind another familiar phrase, from Shakespeare: "Ripeness is all."

below left: Ted Muehling. *Canary and Raven Bird Head Clips.* Scarf clips. 1980. 24-karat gold over bronze, sterling silver. Cast bronze and silver. *Raven:* 2 x 5 x 2″, *Canary:* 2 x 3½ x 2″. Collection the artist. Photograph: Dan Howell

below right: Ted Muehling. *Clam Shell Pins.* 1986. Bronze, oxidized red, 24-karat gold on bronze, sterling silver. Cast. Each 1¾ x 2¼ x ½″. Photograph: Dan Howell

opposite above: Ted Muehling. *Ebony Moth Pendant.* 1988. Ebony, cotton cord. Carved. 2½ x 4 x ½″. Collection the artist. Photograph: Dan Howell

opposite below: Ted Muehling. *Thorn Necklace.* 1987. Oxidized bronze, coral drop. Cast bronze, cut coral. 20 x 2″. Collection the artist. Photograph: Dan Howell

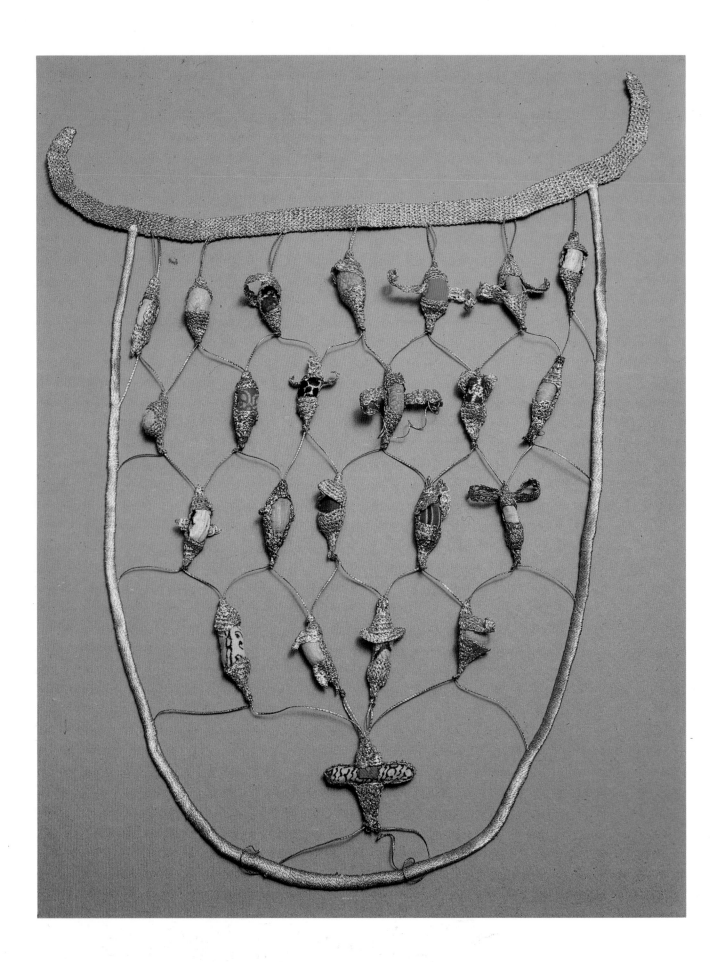

Ruth Nivola

Like the modern-day equivalent of the princess that Rumpelstiltskin set to spinning gold thread, Ruth Nivola has been turning fiber into gold and weaving, crocheting, braiding, twisting, and knotting metallic yarns and vibrant silks into sumptuously rich works.

Though each work requires tens of thousands of stitches, Nivola attends to each stitch individually, treating it as an opportunity to play or experiment. Such an inventive approach comes from the confidence of great dexterity and skill. The result is a captivating web of subtle irregularities. Nivola's open approach to stitching is also tied to her philosophical respect for distinct actions. As Nivola puts it, "Each stitch determines the outcome of the whole. Perhaps it is the same with the world; one drop of water causes the mood of a whole ocean. One single human being, lost in the billions, will shape the spirit of the time."

While Nivola finds inspiration from everything around her, she has been particularly moved by the costumes and baskets of Sardinia, the birthplace of her husband, sculptor Tino Nivola. Nature also provides strong inspiration, as reflected in such titles as *Festival of Queen Bees*. This integration of personal life and art, philosophy and craft adds to the richness of Nivola's work.

opposite: Ruth Nivola. *Festival of Queen Bees.* Neck piece. 1980–81. Silk, metallic yarns. Hammered, stuffed, appliquéd, whipped, knit, crocheted, sewed. 15 x 12½". Collection the artist. Photograph: Noel Rowe

right: Ruth Nivola. *Three Icons.* Neck piece. 1982. Silk, metallic yarns. Crocheted, whipped, hammered. 12½ x 14". Collection the artist. Photograph: Noel Rowe

overleaf left: Ruth Nivola. *Turkish Holiday.* Neck piece. 1985. Silk, metallic yarns. Hammered, stuffed, appliquéd, crocheted, whipped, sewed. 8⅛ x 7¼". Collection the artist. Photograph: Noel Rowe

overleaf right: Ruth Nivola. *Byzantine Seeds.* Neck piece. 1979–80. Silk, metallic yarns. Crocheted, braided, sewed. 26 x 3". Collection the artist. Photograph: Noel Rowe

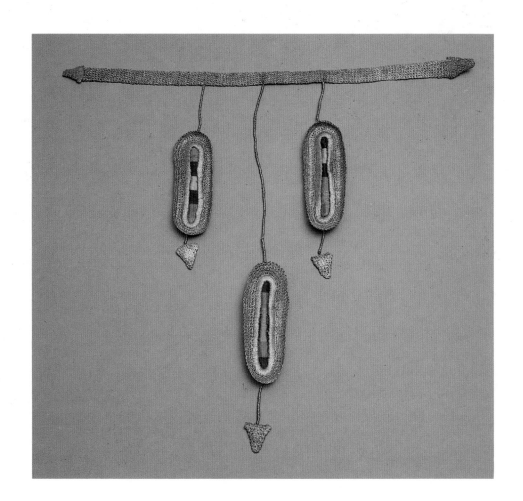

Pavel Opocensky

Pavel Opocensky is in more than one sense a physical jeweler; he is physically engaged with his materials and he demands physical attentiveness on the part of the beholder. In the process of exploring his materials, Opocensky discovers their properties and nuances, making them do the most unexpected and delightful things. In the early 1980s, Opocensky began carving ivory and ebony. He later turned to stone, and it has remained the artist's preferred medium. He has worked it on all scales, from over-life-size monoliths to intimate hand-held objects.

Countering our usual expectations about the properties of stone—hardness, density, roughness—Opocensky reveals more delicate aspects of the material. Instead of dense masses and chunky volumes, he offers transparency and finely tapered edges. Instead of hard unyielding forms, he presents stone's fragility, often working it to the point of breaking. These variations on the material are displayed in tandem, with rough and smooth, thick and thin, solid and transparent coexisting in a single work.

In the late 1980s Opocensky transferred the lessons he learned in stone to the synthetic materials of ColorCore and Surell. Under the artist's hand, these two plastics yielded surprisingly subtle effects. ColorCore, made of layered color laminate, allowed him to create transitions between colored planes, with hues blending and disappearing into one another. A quiet yet palpable excitement occurs when spots of white emerge from layers of red or black, like the visual vibrations of Op art.

Surell, a plastic surrogate for stone, encouraged a similar treatment. Like stone, Surell demands much physical exertion, and Opocensky drills and files the material to create transparent, often weblike surfaces. Opocensky's physical investment in his work is repaid when the viewer or holder—many of his works are designed to be held rather than worn—examines the fine textures of these works.

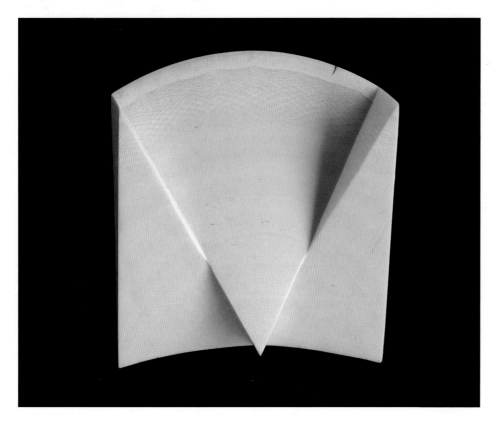

left: Pavel Opocensky. Pin. 1983. Ivory. 3 x 2½ x ½". Photograph: Jan Frank

opposite: Pavel Opocensky. Pin. 1989. Black and white ColorCore. Diam. 4 x ½". Collection Vanessa Lynn, New York. Photograph: Jan Frank

above: Pavel Opocensky. Bracelet. 1993.
ColorCore. Diam. 6 x ³⁄₈″. Photograph:
Martin Tuma

opposite: Pavel Opocensky. Pin. 1989. Red
and white ColorCore. Diam. 4 x ¹⁄₂″.
Photograph: Jan Frank

Joan A. Parcher

Joan Parcher is a smart jeweler. Indeed, "smart" is a word that she repeatedly uses when describing the work of others that she admires. Parcher's admiration is largely reserved for European jewelers, whose work she finds simpler and more thoughtful than that of her American counterparts.

Parcher's own thoughtful approach to jewelry reveals itself in both the format and materials she prefers. One favored format is what the artist calls a "ball and hoop" neck piece. While the weighted element is not always round (it is sometimes a polygon or cone), the form is always geometrical and the solution always elegant.

The works that best convey Parcher's sober yet sensual aesthetic are her graphite pendulums. These neck pieces feature suspended weights made of graphite (the same material used for pencils) hung from steel cables. As the wearer moves, the graphite leaves its mark, gently reminding wearer and viewer that all our actions have consequences. On the other hand, this erosive material is the alter ego of diamond, another carbon-based material.

In addition to offering food for thought, the graphite is simply beautiful. In Parcher's own words, it is "slippery and lustrous." Like all of Parcher's works, these graphite pendulums merge the conceptual and sensual in an understated fashion.

below left: Joan A. Parcher. *Ball and Hoop Neck Piece.* 1989. 23-karat gold leaf over sterling silver, stainless steel cable. Metal construction. 32 x 1⅜". Private collection. Photograph: James Beards

below right: Joan A. Parcher. *Graphite Pendulum-Pendant.* Neck piece. 1990. Soft graphite, sterling silver, stainless steel. Lathe-turned graphite, metal construction. Pendant 1½ x 2 x 1½", cable length 15½". Private collection. Photograph: James Beards

opposite: Joan A. Parcher. *Polka Dot Necklace.* Sterling silver, copper, enamel on copper. Enameled, constructed. 28 x 1 x ½". Private collection. Photograph: Karen Bell

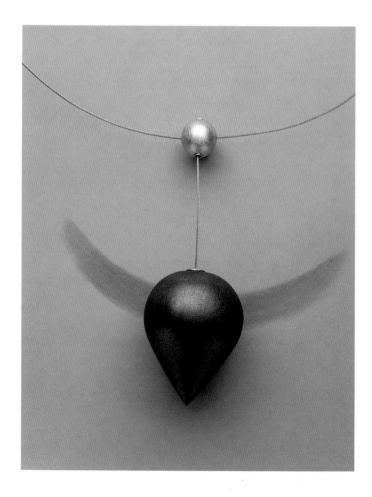

Zack Peabody

Zack Peabody's jewelry allows the wearer to walk around with a little piece of visual security. In a world of random compositions and precarious forms, he offers solidly constructed objects with their structural integrity laid bare. The artist refers to his works as possessing "calculated clarity" and representing "a triumph of the expected over instinct."

To create these eminently predictable and rational works, Peabody uses the strict formal language and materials of engineering—skyscrapers, bridges, and towers. These crowning architectonic structures of humans are a testament to our mastery over the forces of nature: they are structures of proud defiance.

Blatantly manmade, Peabody's works reveal the means of their construction, with bolts, screws, and interlocking strips all evident. Looking like tiny erector-set models, they are tightly fastened in durable metal. While these works are visually opposed to the soft randomness of the human body, they do speak to the human need for security and clear relationships.

left: Zach Peabody. *Brooch 348.* 1993. Stainless steel, niobium. 348 pieces cold-connected using threaded rods. 2¾ x 2¾ x ⅞". Private collection. Photograph: Karen Bell

opposite: Zach Peabody. *Brooch 534.* 1992. Stainless steel, niobium. 534 pieces cold-connected using threaded rods. 1⅞ x 2⅞ x 1". Private collection. Photograph: Karen Bell

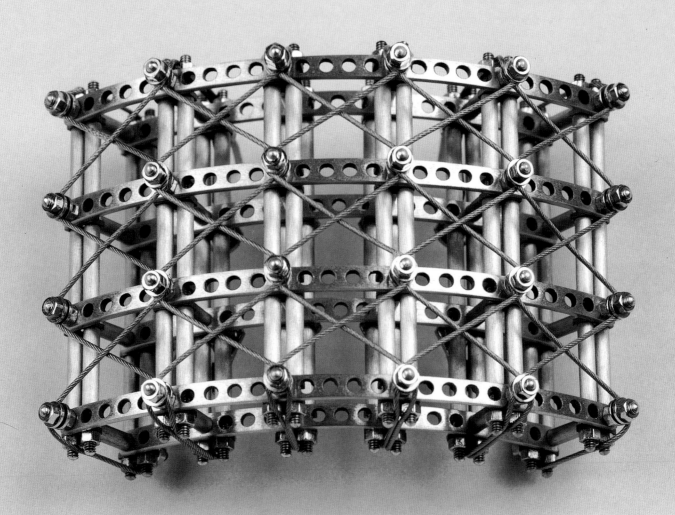

Beverly Penn

Beverly Penn has always been interested in history and the archaeological revival of cultural forms. Many of her brooches have taken the shape of artifacts, including implements, weapons, and amulets. In addition to its role as artifact, Penn also sees the broader cultural function of jewelry as marking important historical and personal events, embodying the memory of marriages, births, and victories. For Penn, jewelry is a container of cultural history.

In recent years Penn has explored this concern through more architectural forms. In the American Southwest, where she has lived for the past decade, Penn is constantly reminded of the history embedded in local customs and structures. Penn carried this sensitivity to historical patterns on a visit to Barcelona, Spain. Her year-long stay in the elaborately wrought city—epitomized by the architecture of Antonio Gaudí—left a distinct impression on her work. Tile roofs, staircases, and window frames began to appear in her brooches, as in *Terraza* of 1990, referring to a Spanish terrace. These architectural fragments are a means of preserving an otherwise hazy past, or, as Penn puts it, "Fragments in the chaos of material culture which we, in the lust of nostalgia, saturate with the poetry of our lives."

below left: Beverly Penn. *Abanico.* Brooch. 1990. Silver, copper, nickel. Fabricated. 4 x 3 x ½". Photograph: Beverly Penn

below right: Beverly Penn. *Terraza.* Brooch. 1990. Silver, copper, nickel. Fabricated. 5 x 1½ x ½". Photograph: Beverly Penn

opposite: Beverly Penn. *For the Roses.* Neck piece. 1991. Copper, 14-karat gold. Fabricated. 11 x 9 x ½". Photograph: David Omer

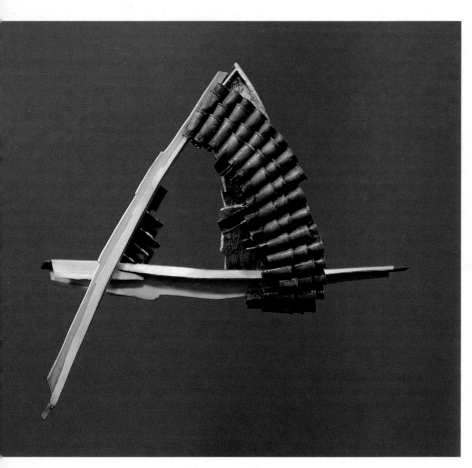

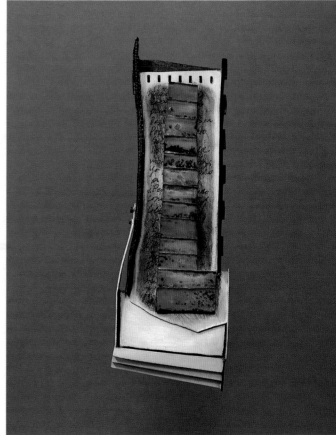

Gene and Hiroko Pijanowski

The works of husband and wife Gene and Hiroko Pijanowski deftly blend two artistic personalities and two distinct cultural backgrounds. Both have spent time in Hiroko's homeland of Japan, and both received Master of Fine Arts degrees from the design-oriented Cranbrook Academy in Michigan. From Japan they acquired several traditional techniques, and from America they derived an innovative and bold approach to materials and form.

Among the traditional Japanese techniques that they have introduced into American jewelry is *sen zogan,* a metal inlay technique, and *mokume-gane,* or wood-grain metal. They spent years on experimentation and research learning to adapt these techniques to their own expressive ends. Since 1984, the Pijanowskis have been exploring the potential of Japanese paper cord, or *mizuhiki,* a traditional material developed over two hundred and fifty years ago. The couple has enlisted this antique material to produce startlingly futuristic works with gleaming metallic finishes and armorlike construction.

In addition to the blend of East and West, old and new, one also finds a combination of reverence and humor in the Pijanowskis' works. In their metalwork series Gentle Solitude, they sought to convey the spirit of Zen Buddhism, creating miniature contemplative universes. On the other hand, their paper cord series bears the title, Oh! I Am Precious, mocking both the status of jewelry and the sanctity of the creator's act.

opposite above: Hiroko Sato Pijanowski and Gene Michael Pijanowski. Neck piece. 1985. *Mizuhiki* (paper cord wrapped with anodized aluminum foil). Glued. 19 x 9 x ¼". Photograph: Gene Pijanowski

opposite below: Hiroko Sato Pijanowski and Gene Michael Pijanowski. *Oh! I Am Precious No. 7.* Edition of 10. Neck piece. 1986. *Mizuhiki* (paper cord wrapped with anodized aluminum foil), canvas, Plexiglas. Glued. 17 x 27 x ½". Photograph: David Kozyra

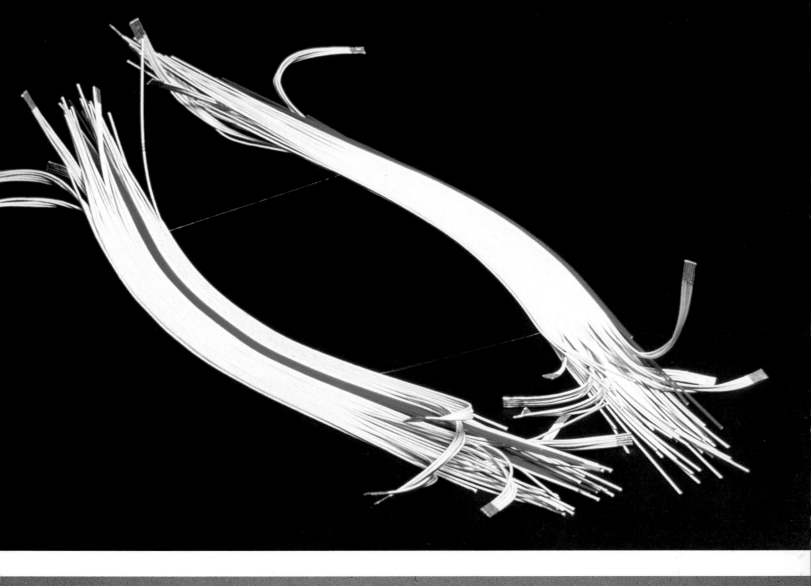

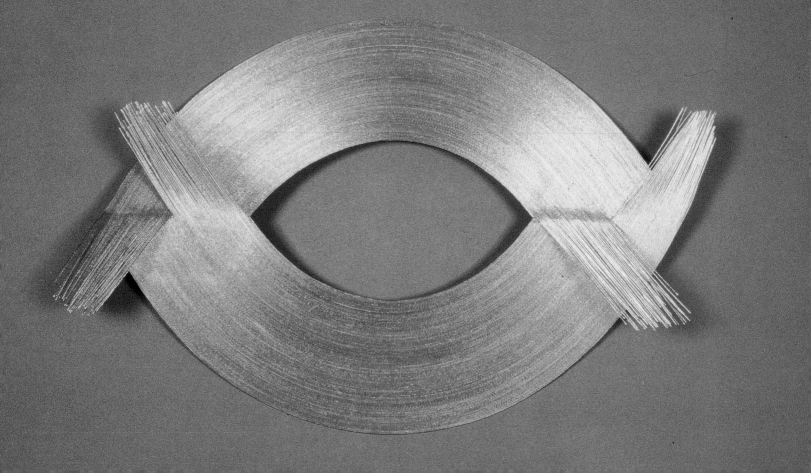

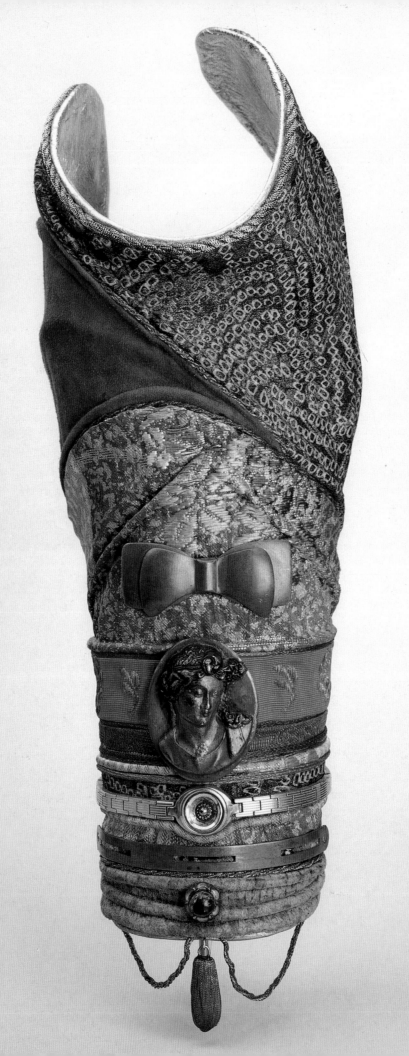

Eric Rhein

Eric Rhein's background in costume design has lent a powerful and striking quality to his jewelry. His previous stage collaborations include costumes for the Joffrey Ballet, the New York City Ballet, and the Imperial Theatre of Tokyo. Both the format and materials of his work assume a theatrical character; he has created cuffs, collars, and codpieces in rich materials such as brocade, silk chiffon, and leather. The resulting pieces are breathtakingly extravagant, recalling the splendor of Elizabethan England or post-Victorian decadence.

Unlike most jewelry, which serves as an accent or punctuation mark resting on the wearer's body, Rhein's works envelop a portion of anatomy. To this extent they are closely allied with costume or fashion, which both conceals and reveals the body beneath it. This dynamic of concealment/revelation is marvelously demonstrated in Rhein's *Cod Piece for Victor.* In this work Rhein turned the codpiece, once a fashion staple in the fifteenth and sixteenth centuries—serving as a protective sheath on men's groins—into a hairy net of protruding wires. Were this piece to be worn, the enclosed member would receive more exposure than protection.

With his fanciful hybrids of fashion and jewelry, Rhein is rather unique in the world of contemporary jewelry. His work gives a new meaning to the term costume jewelry and expands the range of possibilities within the jeweler's repertoire.

opposite: Eric Rhein. *September.* Cuff. 1987. Wire, antique kimono fabrics, antique brocade trim, gold leather, suede, chain, appropriated objects. Glued, constructed. 11 x 5 x 3½". Private collection. Photograph: Jesse Frohman

right: Eric Rhein. *For Victoria.* Cuff. 1990. Wire, kimono fabrics, brocade trim, gold leather, chain, appropriated objects. Glued, constructed. 6 x 5¾ x 5". Private collection. Photograph: Jesse Frohman

overleaf left: Eric Rhein. *Wing.* Pin. 1990. Gold and brass wire, metallic mesh, Japanese kimono fabric, cultured pearls. Glued, constructed. 5½ x 3 x ½". Private collection. Photograph: Jesse Frohman

overleaf right: Eric Rhein. *Destiny.* Bracelet. 1992. Gold, steel, copper, brass and silver wire, appropriated objects. Glued, constructed. 4½ x 3½ x 2¾". Private collection. Photograph: Jesse Frohman

Ondrej Rudavsky

Ondrej Rudavsky enlists his talents as sculptor, painter, and filmmaker to produce quiet yet potent meditative objects. Striving to convey a "mystical feeling" in his work, he heavily develops the surfaces of his small, talismanic forms.

In all sacred cultural objects, a patina suggests not only the passage of time but also the value and use of an object. The thicker and more developed the patina, the more the object was touched and asked to yield its magic power. The warm, rich surfaces that Rudavsky builds on his works, from a mix of beeswax and burnt finishes, give them an aura of the power that accompanies a centuries-old patina.

In addition to the dense surface coating, the suggestive shapes of Rudavsky's works also lend them a sacred overtone. The tapered forms look like ceremonial instruments or symbolic containers. Though their function is questionable, these small objects manage to speak eloquently of the passage of time and the effects of use.

opposite left: Ondrej Rudavsky. *Pin #1.* 1990. Clay. Carved, burned. 6 x ½ x ½". Private collection. Photograph: Gary Keith Griffin

opposite right: Ondrej Rudavsky. *Pin #2.* 1990. Clay. Carved, burned. 6 x ½ x ½". Private collection. Photograph: Gary Keith Griffin

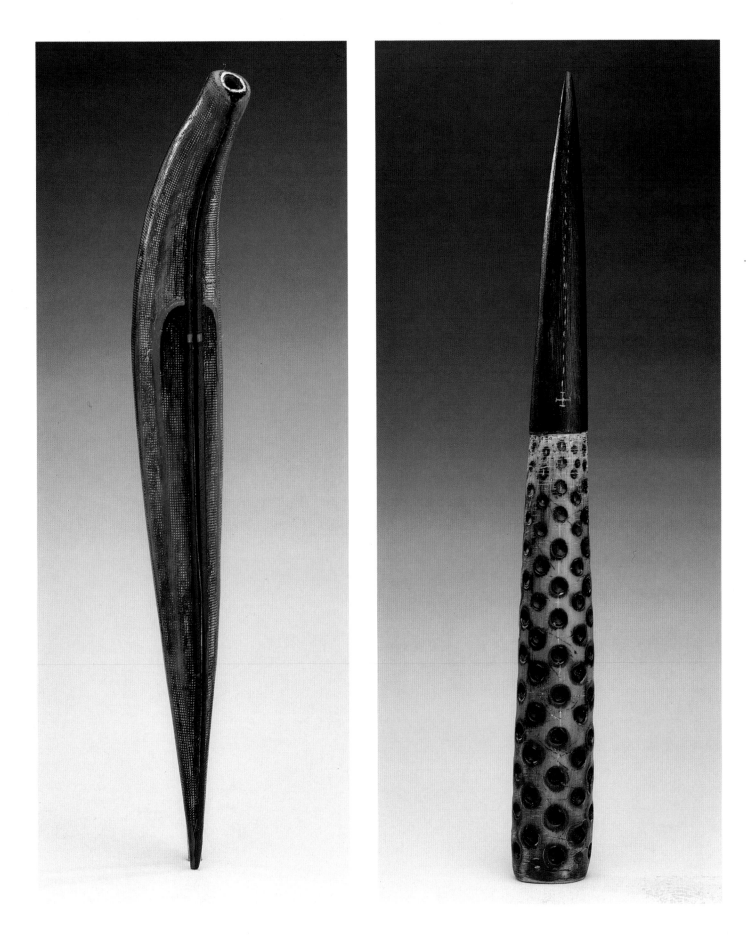

Gayle Saunders

Gayle Saunders's elegant constructions balance dissimilar materials and forms to achieve an exquisite tension. Working primarily in the brooch format, the artist typically couples a black steel armature with an irregular gold shape suspended within. The starkness and geometry of the outer structure contrasts with the broken and organic character of the precious material inside. In the brooch *A Quiet Place,* for example, a tattered square of gold is tightly strung within a steel circle; pulled with wire from four corners, it looks like a victim about to be flayed.

The tensions in Saunders's work ultimately resolve into a delicate balance of opposites through the artist's restrained means and attention to process, which reflect the Japanese aesthetic that Saunders cites as her inspiration. The titles of her works underline this connection to Japanese culture. *Introspection, Focused,* and *A Quiet Place* conjure associations of contemplation and meditation, pointing to the artist's involvement with the philosophy of Zen. Saunders's subtle works encourage a meditative response from the viewer, acting as a focal point for contemplation.

below: Gayle Saunders. *Rebirth.* Brooch. 1988. 18-karat yellow gold with 14-karat colored golds, steel. Fused, fabricated, forged, partially rusted. 1 x 3½ x ¾". Private collection. Photograph: Ralph Gabriner

opposite above: Gayle Saunders. *Crossroads.* Brooch. 1989. Steel, 14- and 18-karat gold. Forged, fabricated, partially rusted. Diam. 2¼ x ⅜". Private collection. Photograph: Ralph Gabriner

opposite below: Gayle Saunders. *A Quiet Place.* Brooch. 1987. 18-karat yellow gold with 14-karat colored golds, steel. Fused, rolled, fabricated. Diam. 4 x 3¼". Collection Frederica Miceli, New York. Photograph: Ralph Gabriner

Joyce Scott

Joyce Scott is proud of her heritage as the daughter of sharecroppers and rural artisans. Her grandmother, grandfather, aunt, and mother all made quilts and practiced other domestic arts. Scott's heritage has influenced her choice of medium and her belief that art and life should be integrated. Scott strives to achieve spiritual satisfaction through her work. "I pour so much of myself into my work," says Scott. "Most artists hide behind their work, I expose myself in it."

Scott's work could not be further from the notion of jewelry as decorative adornment. Typically narrative, her pieces run the gamut from political outrage to personal whimsy. They always carry a social message, even if it is tempered by humor or irony. She has tackled subjects such as the Holocaust, slavery, social injustice, sexual abuse, voyeurism, and jealousy. The work encourages social responsibility and reminds us of the harmful things that are happening all around us.

The rich social import of Scott's work is matched by its visual richness. Scott describes her beadwork as a cross between sculpture and painting. The artist treats the beads like the dabs of paint in a Pointillist canvas, but unlike paint (a medium Scott has tried), glass beads have the advantage of being translucent and can both capture and reflect light. Scott's virtuoso weaving technique—a method similar to crochet called the peyote stitch, which she learned from a Cree Indian—allows great fluidity of form, resulting in protruding hollow forms and undulating effects. Scott is always seeking greater technical challenges; her work has grown increasingly more daring and dazzling in its visual richness and range of subject matter.

below left: Joyce Scott. *The Sneak.* Neck piece. 1989. Beads, thread. Beadwork. 13½ x 11 x 5½". Private collection. Photograph: Kanji Takeno

below right: Joyce Scott. *Adam and Eve.* Neck piece. 1985. Beads, thread. Beadwork. 10 x 8 x 1½". Collection D. Schneier, New York. Photograph: Noel Allum Photography

opposite: Joyce Scott. *Hunger.* Neck piece. 1991. Beads, thread, photographs, plastic. Beadwork. Approx. 17 x 13 x ¼". Collection Mint Museum of Art, Charlotte, N.C. Photograph: Kanji Takeno

Sandra Sherman

Sandra Sherman creates kinetic jewelry that changes its structure and volume as the wearer moves. These pieces, mostly bracelets, are constructed to be flexible and adjustable, allowing for diverse possibilities. The artist has said that she intends the interaction between wearer and piece to encourage an attitude of "serious play."

The artist has explored the kinetic possibilities of jewelry in three series, each based on a different structural element. Her first series, which she calls the Chain Mail series, is composed of wire and metal rings linked together to form a netlike web that collapses and extends upon moving. The second series is built around hinged elements and allows for more dramatic movement. On bending the arm or wrist, the wearer produces a hollow form with increased volume. Sherman's third series, exploring the interplay between motion and structural change, is based on fringelike pieces attached to a central ring. The loose fringe elements move in a fluid fashion without settling into a single structure.

Like chameleons, the works in the three series change their shape and character based on the wearer's cues. In this way Sherman's jewelry underlines the symbiotic relationship between wearer and object, setting up a kinetic dialogue between the two.

Most recently, Sherman has embarked on a more traditional, less interactive exploration of the medium. Her latest work enlists such materials as crystal chandelier parts to create pendants that are conventional, though uncommonly beautiful.

Sandra Sherman. *Sun Hinge Bracelet* (open and compressed) 1988. Gold-plated brass. Constructed. Diam. compressed 5$\frac{1}{2}$ x 1$\frac{1}{4}$". Private collection. Photograph: Jochen Grün

Sandra Sherman. Necklace. 1987. Mother-of-pearl and glass buttons, iron wire. Constructed. 12½ x 3 x ¾". Private collection. Photograph: Jochen Grün

Sandra Sherman. *Samson and Delilah.* "Diptych" necklace. 1990. Sterling silver, nickel, lead crystal, beads, old chandelier crystal. Constructed, patina. 16 x 1". Private collection. Photograph: Jochen Grün

Kiff Slemmons

Using recognizable forms as a point of departure, Kiff Slemmons explores the poetic and ambiguous nature of the everyday world. The artist strives "to make something of utmost clarity with questions still inside it." In her desire to create evocative works, Slemmons is closely aligned with the aims of earlier Symbolist and Surrealist artists.

Beginning with common images, such as hands or birds, Slemmons plays with various materials and meanings to yield a number of different associations. She has found the serial format ideal for such an approach, as it permits the artist to expand an idea and develop variations on a theme. One such series is Hands of the Heroes of 1989. Cultural figures such as Martin Luther King, Jacques Cousteau, Emily Dickinson, and Marcel Proust are depicted by means of symbolic clues that provide a concise visual metaphor for their personalities. For example, Martin Luther King is portrayed as an ebony and ivory hand stitched together with copper wire, and Marcel Proust is symbolized by a clock with wobbly hands, creating a visual pun of hands within a hand.

The Hands series evolved into a series of Cages, in which Slemmons characteristically played with the links between a rib cage, a bird cage, and prison cells. *Figure Out,* an unsettling piece in the series, displays the word *out* caged in the chest of an amputated figure, suggesting a condition of containment or frustrated communication.

The intimate scale of jewelry is perfectly suited to the poetic and intricate content of Slemmons's work. She herself has stated, "The realm of the small is where I want to be. I like taking large ideas and making them small."

opposite: Kiff Slemmons. *Cool.* Brooch. 1989. Sterling silver. Fabricated. 2¼ x 2¼ x ³⁄₈″. Collection Marcella Benditt, Seattle. Photograph: Rod Slemmons

right: Kiff Slemmons. *Figure Out.* Brooch. 1990. Sterling silver, acrylic. Fabricated. 2½ x 4½ x ¼″. Collection Marvin and Yolanda Stein, Seattle. Photograph: Rod Slemmons

overleaf left: Kiff Slemmons. *Hands of the Heroes: Roald Amundsen.* Brooch. 1987. Sterling silver, acrylic. Fabricated. 3 x 2½ x ½″. Collection Mark Del Vecchio, New York. Photograph: Rod Slemmons

overleaf right: Kiff Slemmons. *Hands of the Heroes: Stephen Jay Gould.* Brooch. 1989. Copper, Japanese metalwork. Fabricated. 3 x 2½ x ³⁄₁₆″. Collection the artist. Photograph: Rod Slemmons

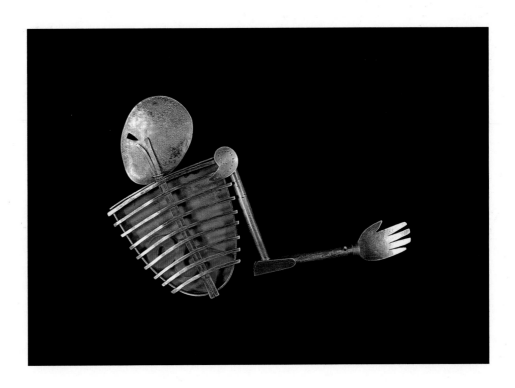

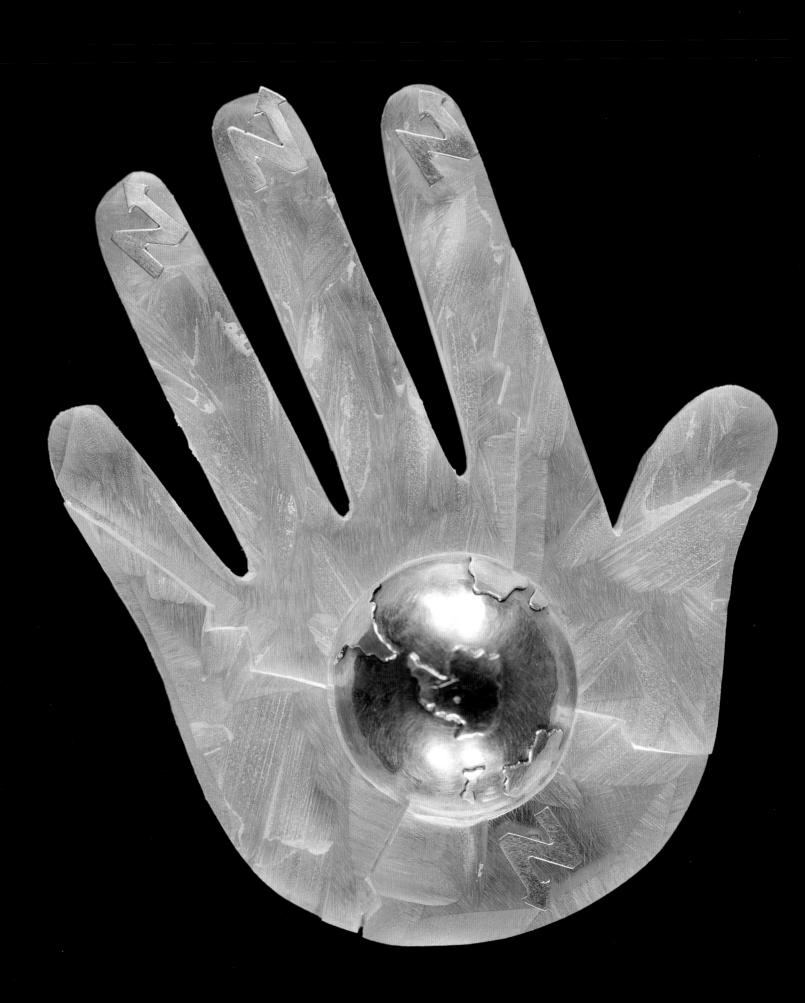

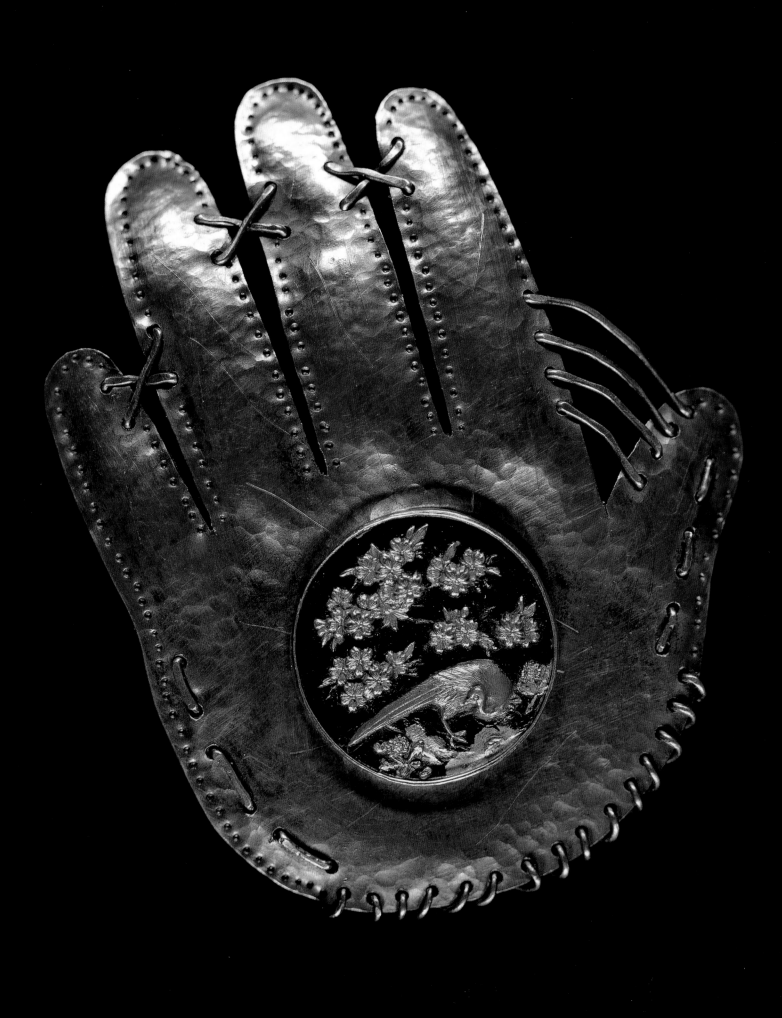

Jill Slosburg-Ackerman

For anyone who has given it any thought, it is clear that the term *earring* is totally inadequate as a description of ear jewelry, since very few of the things that hang from our lobes actually take the shape of rings. Jill Slosburg-Ackerman has carried this examination of ear ornamentation a step further, going on to question our habit of pairing identical objects on each lobe. While many people have casually played with the idea of lobal asymmetry—wearing only one earring or mixing different earrings—Slosburg-Ackerman exploits the earring format to conduct a more rigorous analysis of the nature of duality.

This interest is clearly stated in the title of her series Living in Two Worlds. According to the artist, this series attempts to reconcile many of the dualities in her own life, including that between artist and teacher, jeweler and sculptor, and woman and citizen. In addition to these more personal associations it also addresses larger pairs, such as solid and void, male and female. Slosburg-Ackerman explores such dualities in the brooch format as well, juxtaposing two different elements within the confines of a single frame.

Another recurring motif that preoccupies the artist is that of the vessel. The vessel form allows her to further pursue her interest in duality, with the play of inside and outside, mass and space, open and closed. Negative space also figures in her hollow wire works, which are wrapped around a thin column of space.

left: Jill Slosburg-Ackerman. *Living in Two Worlds.* Brooch. 1990. Shibuichi. Cast, fabricated. 2 x 2½ x ¼". Collection James Sloss Ackerman, Cambridge, Mass. Photograph: Stanley Rowin

opposite: Jill Slosburg-Ackerman. *Living in Two Worlds.* Earrings. 1981. Sterling silver. Fabricated. 1½ x ½ x ½". Private collection. Photograph: Kay Canavino

above: Jill Slosburg-Ackerman. *Terra Firma.* Bracelet. 1989. Ebony, pigment. Carved. 3 x 3³/₄ x ⁷/₈". Private collection. Photograph: Stanley Rowin

opposite: Jill Slosburg-Ackerman. *Living in Two Worlds.* Pair of earrings in three parts (the wearer leaves one behind). 1990. Maple, ebony, pigment, metal. Carved, engraved. Left and right 1¹/₂ x ³/₄ x ³/₄"; center diam. 1¹/₂ x ¹/₈". Private collection. Photograph: Stanley Rowin

Christina Smith

Most jewelry derives its intimacy from its small scale and wearability, but the intimacy of Christina Smith's jewelry comes from its content as well. According to the artist, "Each piece is based on a moment of my personal history." These memories are frozen in sterling silver and comprise a wearable diary of the artist's life.

While Smith's brooches can be called narrative, they seem to be vignettes rather than complete stories. Like rebuses or puzzles, they have a few visual elements—a figure, object, animal—set in geometric frames. Not fully contained by their frames or stages, the elements often protrude or dangle, creating visual tension.

The placement of the figures and objects provides one clue to the drama in these works. Colored acrylic accents, typically in red, add to the interest. While it is hard to tell a story in only one frame, these vignettes manage to convey action and drama. They are pregnant little moments that can be worn on one's chest.

When the subject matter comes from the evening news or more public events, the meaning of these narrative brooches still remains unclear. Like much modern art, Smith's work raises more questions than it answers. Its interest lies in this ability to keep us guessing.

below left: Christina Smith. *Just a Minute Maud.* Brooch. 1989. Sterling silver and acrylic. Fabricated silver, roller-printed. 3 x 4″. Private collection. Photograph: Dave Devries

below right: Christina Smith. *Scanga's Emergency.* Brooch. 1988. Sterling silver and acrylic. Fabricated silver, roller-printed. 4 x 4″. Collection The Oakland Museum, Calif. Photograph: Dave Devries

opposite: Christina Smith. *Jack Is Expensive.* Brooch. 1989. Sterling silver, acrylic. Fabricated silver, roller-printed. 3 x 2½″. Collection Susan Kingsley, Carmel Valley. Photograph: Dave Devries.

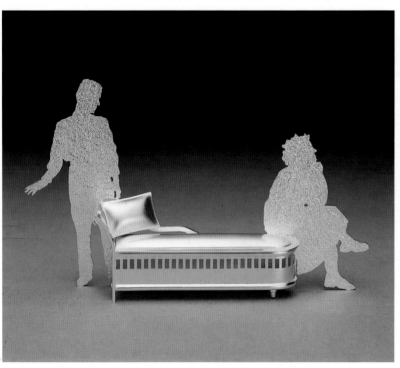

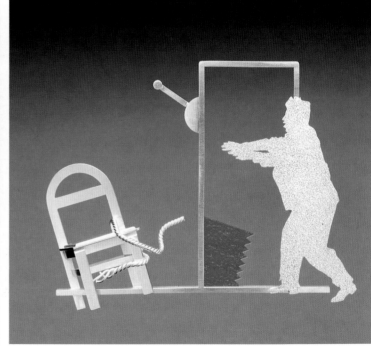

Lisa Spiros

Strength, hardness, and cold determination—these qualities spring to mind when one thinks of steel. These same properties characterize Lisa Spiros's work, and it is no coincidence that steel is her favored material. This rather cold and sober material suits her direct, matter-of-fact objects.

Clearly uninterested in merely adorning or enhancing the wearer in her work, Spiros seeks to make simple, reductivist forms, shunning all extraneous effects or material excess. Through gradual reduction and paring away, she is left with plain, almost archetypal forms—compact material facts. They were all left untitled to underscore the physical stubbornness of these works.

Rather than striving to make a statement, in many ways Spiros creates anti-statements, little voids of mute objects that the wearer fills with associations or meaning. Spiros's negative, reductive aesthetic denies the traditional aspects of jewelry in order to assert the strength of hard, clean form. The artist states, "Raw form is the essential expression; material is the vehicle in making the statement."

Like Minimalist sculpture of the 1970s, Spiros's works seem impersonal and unengaged, yet they have an undeniable presence and magnetic pull. As Diana Vreeland, the celebrated fashion maven, observed, "Elegance is refusal, and refusal is seductive."

below right: Lisa Spiros. Pendant. 1992. Stainless steel sheet and cable. Formed, soldered construction. 1⁹/₁₆ x 2¹/₂ x ³/₄". Private collection. Photograph: Karen Bell

below left: Lisa Spiros. Pendant. 1990. Stainless steel sheet and cable. Metal construction, oil patina. 2¹/₂ x 2¹/₂ x ¹/₈". Collection Clodagh, New York. Photograph: Rebekah Laskin

opposite: Lisa Spiros. Bracelet. 1992. Stainless steel mesh. Formed, folded, soldered construction. 2¹/₂ x 3 x 3". Private collection. Photograph: Karen Bell

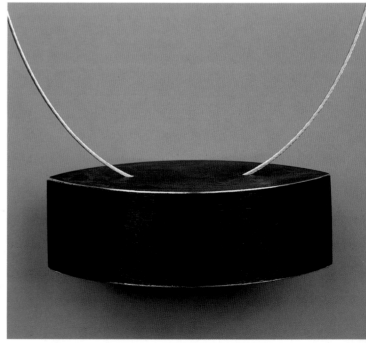

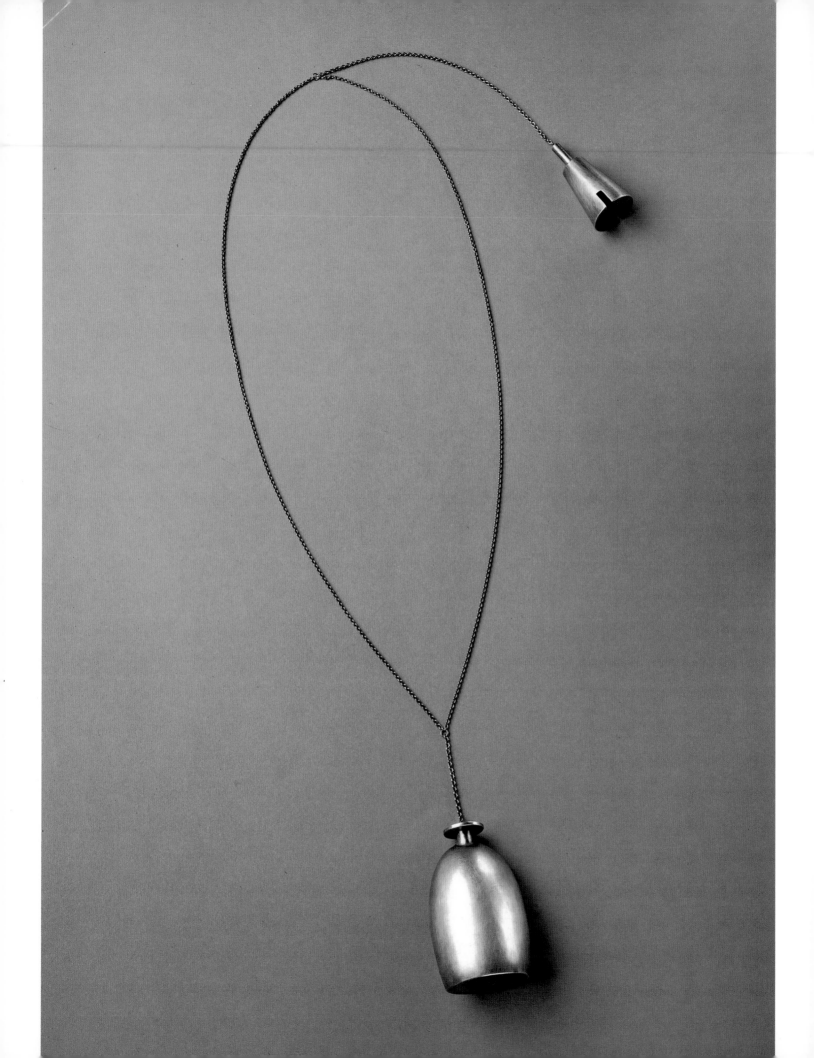

Didi Suydam

opposite and below: Didi Suydam.
Pendant/Object (open and closed). 1992.
Oxidized sterling silver. Hollow formed,
fabricated. 4 x 1⅝ x 1¼". Collection Susan
Hoagland, Corte Madera. Photograph:
Roger Birn

below right: Didi Suydam. Brooch. 1990.
Sterling silver, 23-karat gold leaf. Hollow-
formed, fabricated. 3 x 3 x ½". Photograph: Roger Birn

About her approach to jewelry, Didi Suydam has stated, "Fundamentally, I see the body as a vast open space, an empty landscape." Suydam's finely wrought constructions, with their strong structural integrity and articulation of interior and exterior space, could be likened to miniature body architecture.

On first impression, Suydam's works may look uncomplex and uninteresting. On further consideration, however, they reveal themselves to be powerfully evocative little constructions. Though her forms are simplified, they echo other more resonant forms, such as arches, urns, arrows, and windows. In their stylization, these shapes take on the aspect of archetypal symbols that stand for no one thing in particular but many things in general. Rather than a liability, this lack of specificity proves to be Suydam's strength.

In addition to the associations that these works trigger, with their meticulous craftsmanship and rich materials like sterling silver, alabaster, and ebony, they also provide visual satisfaction. The recurring incisions in the hollow forms add yet another element of interest, laying bare the wearer's body beneath the work.

Rachelle Thiewes

Above all, Rachelle Thiewes's jewelry is theatrical; it transforms the wearer into a performer and everyday attire into costume. While most jewelry is designed to call attention to the body in one way or another, Thiewes's works do so explicitly and strongly, thereby making unusual demands on the wearer.

Several aspects of the jewelry conspire to produce its highly active and interactive nature. A recurring form in Thiewes's structural vocabulary is a sharply tapered cone with the distinct potential for poking or jabbing. Though ultimately harmless, the inherent danger of these spiky forms keeps both wearer and viewer alert. They are thus prodded into consciousness, made aware of the implications of their body movements: every movement has a consequence; no gesture is gratuitous.

The element of sound also contributes to the wearer's awareness. Many of the various cone and disk structures are strung together like beads or chimes, creating sound as the body moves. The effect may be rhythmic and musical, or it may be irregular and elusive. Thiewes's sensitivity to jewelry's musical dimension is not surprising, given that she is married to a jazz musician and turns to music as a major source of inspiration. The titles of her works underline the importance of music and performance, for example, *Uptown Dance, Silent Dance,* and *Grappelli Bracelet,* after the musician Stephen Grapelli.

Unlike a lot of "wearer-friendly" jewelry, Thiewes's work requires attention and intelligence from a wearer. However, like most difficult things, it rewards one with understanding and knowledge. In this sense, Thiewes's work is didactic; it serves to educate us about the motion and rhythm of our bodies.

below: Rachelle Thiewes. Bracelet. 1988. Silver, 18-karat gold, slate. Hollow construction, carved slate, heat, chemical color. 3½ x 14 x 12″. Private collection. Photograph: Rachelle Thiewes

opposite left: Rachelle Thiewes. *Uptown Dance Series.* Brooch. 1986. Silver, 18-karat gold. Hollow construction, heat, chemical color. 8 x 1¼ x ¾″. Private collection. Photograph: Russell Banks

opposite right: Rachelle Thiewes. *Wire Pin.* 1986. Silver, 18-karat gold, carved slate. Hollow construction, heat, chemical color. 8½ x 1½ x 1½″. Collection Adair Margo, El Paso. Photograph: Russell Banks

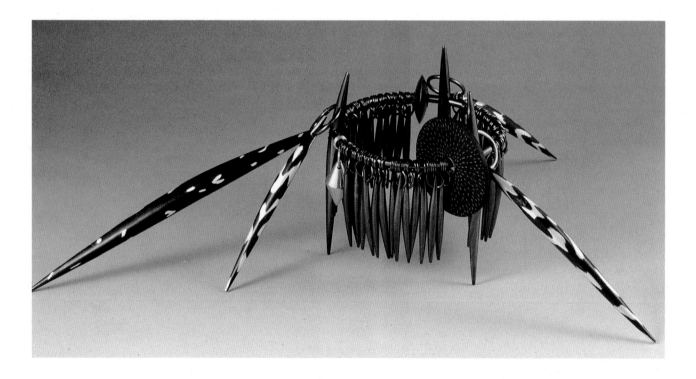

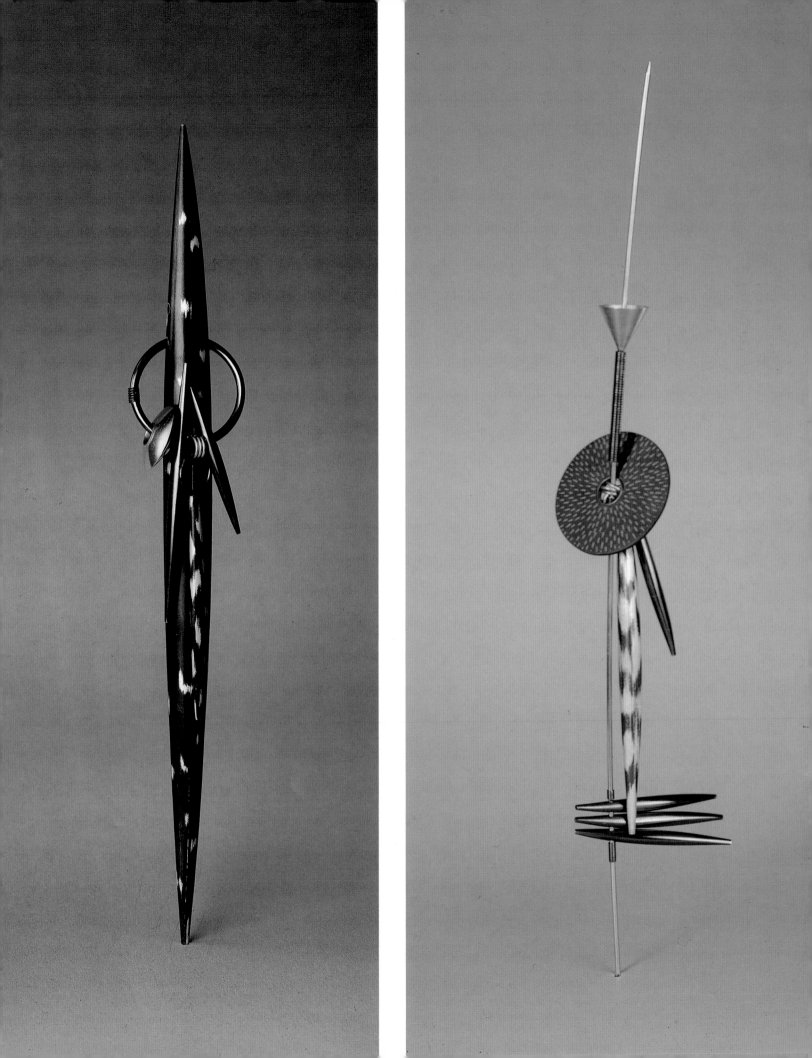

Alan Burton Thompson

It is not incidental that Alan Burton Thompson worked as a professional magician for five years before devoting himself more fully to jewelry. His enigmatic collaged compositions are filled with optical illusions and narrative sleights of hand.

Working in the brooch format, Burton Thompson enlists a rich assortment of materials to produce his optical tricks. One can find pearls and plastic, velvet and coral, felt and glitter, all conjoined in layered compositions. The layering produces a sense of illusion, while the fragmented narratives lend a touch of mystery and magic.

Suggestive titles like *Balance, Grace,* and *Hoop Ghost* may provide a clue to the artist's thoughts, but these works ultimately remain elusive. Even with recurring motifs like cameo heads or bladelike shapes, one can never be secure about the intended meaning or connection. The viewer is left to wonder how Burton Thompson's tricks are done and even why they were done in this combination.

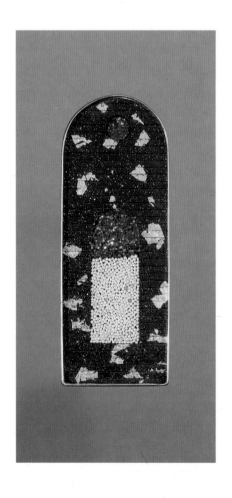

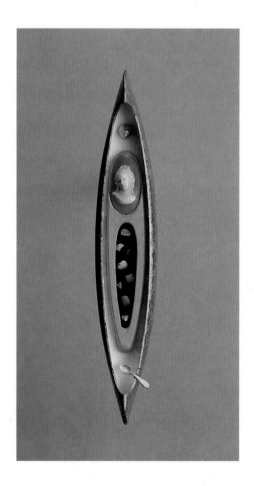

far left: Alan Burton Thompson. *Window.* Brooch. 1988. Sterling silver, acrylic, plastic, paint, glitter, glass beads. Constructed. 2½ x 1 x ¼″. Collection Sean Licka, Fairbanks, Alaska. Photograph: Robert Hirsch III

left: Alan Burton Thompson. *Boat.* Brooch. 1987. Plastic, basswood, opals, brass, 22-karat gold leaf, cameo, shell. Constructed. 7½ x 1¼ x 1″. Collection Yoshiko Yamamoto, Boston. Photograph: Robert Hirsch III

opposite: Alan Burton Thompson. *Hoop Ghost.* Brooch. 1989. Basswood, cameo, glass, shell, 24-karat gold plate, paint, sterling silver, synthetic ruby. Constructed. 5 x 1¼ x ½″. Collection Jamie Bennett, New Paltz, N.Y. Photograph: Robert Hirsch III

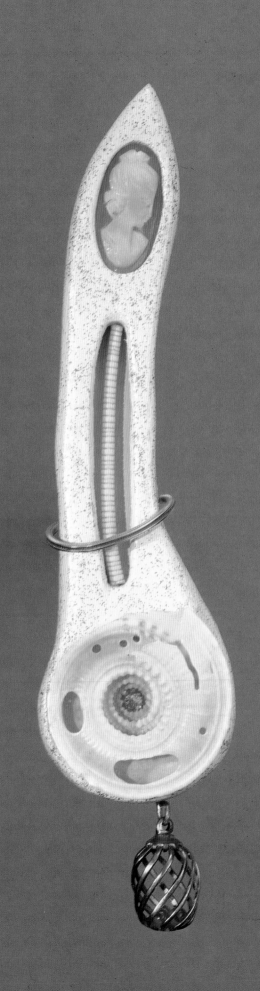

Cathryn Vandenbrink

Cathryn Vandenbrink's work reenacts the different eras of human history, from the Bronze Age to the Iron Age to the modern age of steel and rubber. While she retains a similar form throughout her work—a hollow tapered fibulalike tube—she lends these forms different characteristics through the use of various metals and patinas.

The titles of her works bear out the historical range of her references—from *Shard Earrings* to *UFO Earrings,* ancient artifacts to futuristic spaceships. Vandenbrink's influences are just as diverse as her subjects, and she draws inspiration from many ethnic groups and periods.

Vandenbrink uses metals as if she were wielding a palette of color and historical associations; silver and gold suggest cultural refinement, while reddish copper implies a more primitive age. Rusted metal holds a particular place in her works, not only because it lends color but because it also speaks of the corrosive passage of time. Within the narrow artistic range that Vandenbrink has mapped out for herself, she is still able to convey the expressive properties of materials.

Cathryn Vandenbrink. Necklace. 1991. Steel, iron, copper, rubber. Fabricated, assembled. 1¼ x 7 x ½". Private collection. Photograph: Richard Nicol

Cathryn Vandenbrink. Brooch. 1991.
Steel. Fabricated. 2½ x 4½ x ½". Collection Marcella Benditt, Seattle. Photograph:
Richard Nicol

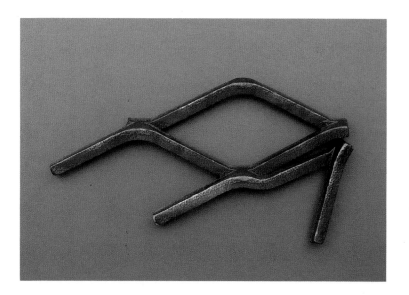

Cathryn Vandenbrink. Necklace and hollow forms. 1990. Copper, sterling silver, rubber. Fabricated. Necklace 6¾ x ⅜ x ⅜". Photograph: Richard Nicol

Barbara Walter

On first impression, Barbara Walter's rings appear to be humorous finger toys. The artist intentionally uses such humor as the "hook" to arouse the viewer's interest. Walter also finds that jewelry's small scale serves to "draw people in," captivating them like a whisper.

On getting closer and examining these intricate little sculptures, the viewer discovers more than humor. The works are usually built around a verbal pun, as in *Gopher Broke Wheel of Fortune Ring Toy,* which warns of the risks of gambling. Other works, like *Three Ring Circus with Ringmaster,* also go beyond mere amusement. A tense undertone is created by the ringmaster, whose whip drives the cogs supporting the circus performers. The circular format of the ring is often used to suggest vicious circles or relentless pursuits.

Though most of Walter's rings are not designed to be worn, their movable parts encourage physical engagement. Like tiny toys, these works often have a puzzle that asks to be solved, further challenging the viewer to become involved.

below left: Barbara Walter. *Steeplechase Horse Race Ring Toy.* 1983. Sterling silver, brass, plastic. Cast, fabricated. 2 x 1 x ½". Private collection. Photograph: Tom Prutisto

below right: Barbara Walter. *Gopher Broke Wheel of Fortune Ring Toy.* 1984. Sterling silver, brass, copper, plastic. Cast, fabricated, machined. 1½ x 1 x ½". Photograph: Tom Prutisto

opposite: Barbara Walter. *Three Ring Circus with Ringmaster.* Ring. 1977. Sterling silver, 14-karat gold, brass. Cast, fabricated. 2 x 2 x 1". Private collection. Photograph: Tom Prutisto

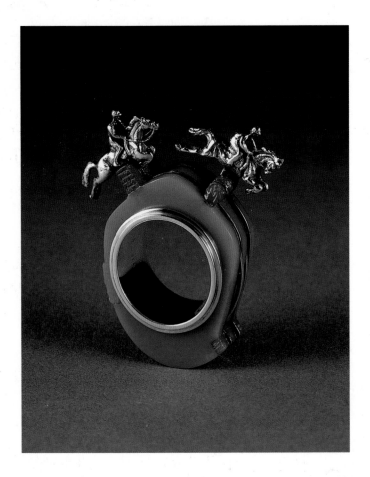

Joe Wood

Joe Wood began his artistic career as a sculptor, producing large outdoor works. This sculptural background is evident in his jewelry, which is intimately involved with issues of structure and space. Wood shifted to the small-scale, wearable format in order to better control the elements of his work and to engage the wearer's body.

Traditionally, sculpture has concerned itself with mass and space, solid and void, and Wood is clearly occupied with these concerns. His interest in space is so developed that one could even talk about the architectural quality of Wood's works. They not only suggest or displace space, they actually contain space and even provide shelter for other objects. This architectural aspect can be found in his series of cagelike brooches, most notably the *Shell Brooch* of 1988. Here, a beautifully engineered shell—itself once an animal shelter—is contained in the equally measured and controlled cage of the artist.

Control, measure, and rule are the hallmarks of Wood's art. One pictures him, compass in hand, drawing and redrawing ideal proportions and relationships. His draftsmanship and engineering mind are evident in the *Drawing Series Brooch*. Like Vitruvius, who attempted to circumscribe man in a circle and square, Wood enlists jewelry to mark off and add structure to the human form.

below left: Joe Wood. *Black Brooch with Shell.* 1988. Brass, black nickel plate, shell, nylon. Constructed. 2¼ x 2¼ x ½". Photograph: Dean Powell

below right: Joe Wood. *Drift.* Brooch. 1992. Sterling silver, 18-karat yellow gold, graphite, nylon. Constructed, smoked oil patina. 2 x 4 x ½". Photograph: Dean Powell

opposite: Joe Wood. *Through-Point.* Brooch. 1991. Sterling silver, graphite. Constructed, smoked oil patina. 2½ x 2½ x 1¾". Photograph: Dean Powell

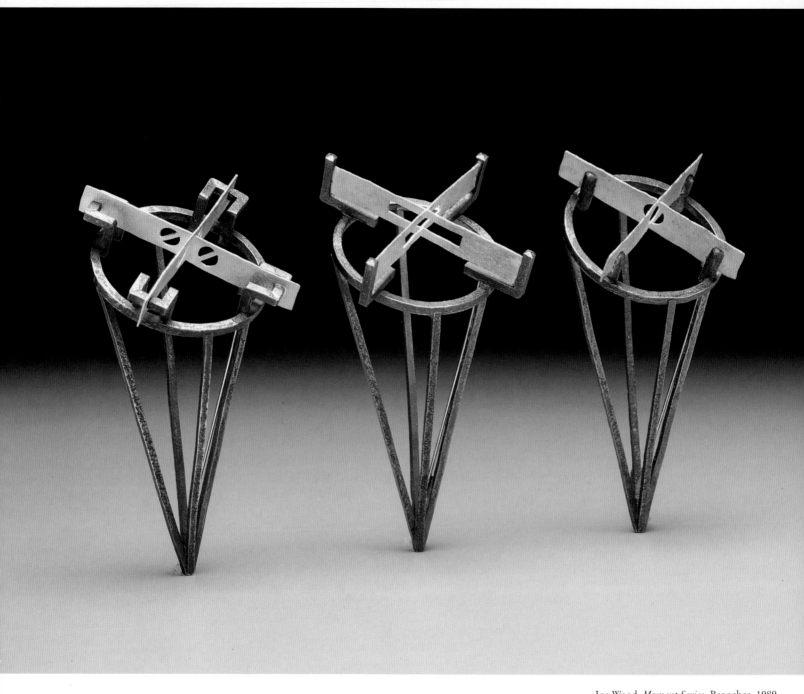

Joe Wood. *Moment Series.* Brooches. 1989.
Oxidized sterling silver, 18-karat gold.
Constructed. Each 3 x 1 x 1″. Photograph:
Dean Powell

Joe Wood. *November Series.* Three
brooches. 1992. Copper, brass, bronze,
sterling. Constructed. Each 2 x 3 x ¾".
Photograph: Dean Powell

Glossary

Anodizing The use of electrical current to create a porous structure on the surface of aluminum. This coarse skin can be colored and sealed, creating a surface that is durable and nonconductive.

Armlet A work held in place by slight pressure of the body itself. It is worn anywhere from just above the wrist bone to above the biceps.

Bracelet A work worn loosely above the wrist.

Bronze An alloy of copper and tin, favored for centuries for casting. In modern use, brasses with a golden color are often called bronze.

Brooch Derived from the French *broche,* "a spit or skewer." An ornamental clasp of various forms, originally having a tongue, now a pin or loop, by which it can be fastened onto a garment.

Casting The process of pouring or injecting molten metal into a mold to create a desired form.

Cold connection Any method of constructing a work that does not use solder, which by definition requires heat.

Coloring The natural, chemical, or heat patination of metal.

Die forming A large family of techniques that use forms made of a hard material to impose a predetermined contour on sheet metal.

Electroforming A technique in which metal is electrolytically deposited onto a conductive matrix.

Electroplating *See* plating.

Émail en résille sur verre Literally, enamel in network on glass, executed by carving a design in slightly concave depressions on a plaque of glass (usually dark green or blue green) or crystal. The depressions are then lined with gold leaf and filled with powdered transparent colored enamels.

Fabricated In jewelry making, constructed by assembling parts or sections.

Fibula A decorative fastener used by ancient cultures to secure clothing. A forerunner to the kilt pin and safety pin.

Forging The process of shaping metal with a hammer.

Fusing The joining of pieces of metal by melting adjacent areas together, that is, using heat without the addition of solder.

Hollowware The generic term applied to containers. Hollowware can be made by machine or with hand tools.

Karat The measure used to express the purity of gold, 24 karat being the highest or purest. An alloy of half pure gold and half another metal would be expressed as 12 karat.

opposite: John Iversen. Nine bracelets. 1978–80. Oxidized brass, bronze, copper, metal alloys, nickel. Fabricated, tension-formed. Each 3 x 7 x ½″. Collection the artist. Photograph: Karen Bell

Marriage of metals   In this process, a flat sheet of metal is pierced by a saw. Into the opening a second metal of the same shape and size is inserted and soldered.

Mokume   In this Japanese technique, layers of metal are laminated together and then cut to expose the inner striations. The word translates as "wood grain," which describes one effect of the process.

Nickel silver   Also German silver. An alloy of approximately 65 percent copper, 17 percent zinc, and 18 percent nickel. Similar in properties, cost, and workability to brass, and familiar from the American five-cent coin.

Niello   A lustrous black inlay made of silver, lead, copper, and sulfur.

Niobium   A reactive metal that, like titanium, has become popular in jewelry making. A range of bright colors can be achieved by creating thin layers of oxides through electrolytic oxide formation.

Patina   A surface coloration on metal achieved either naturally, through exposure to the atmosphere, or artificially, through the application of oxides, carbonates, or sulfides.

Plating   An electrolytic process in which a thin layer of metal is deposited onto a conductive surface.

Refractory metals   Metals that have an extremely high melting point—one above that of iron or nickel.

Rivet   A short piece of metal, typically wire, that penetrates through two or more pieces of metal and is peened (flattened with a hammer) on each end to secure the layers in place.

Roll printing   A technique in which sheet metal is passed between steel rollers under great pressure and in contact with a textured or patterned material, thereby transferring an impression of the texture or pattern onto the metal.

Shakudo   A copper alloy (97–75 percent copper and 3–25 percent pure gold) widely used in the arts in Japan.

Shibuichi   A copper alloy (75 percent copper and 25 percent silver) widely used in the arts in Japan and well suited to *mokume* laminates.

Stamping   A simple technique in which steel punches are used to imprint an image or pattern into metal. Stamping is also used to mark the quality and maker of an object.

Torque, torc, or torch   A stiff, twisted collar or necklace with an opening at the back.

Bibliography

American Craft Council. *Jewelry U.S.A.* New York, 1984

Blauer, Ettagale, ed. *Contemporary American Jewelers.* New York: Van Nostrand Reinhold, 1991

Bury, Shirley. *Jewellery: 1789–1910, the International Era.* Wappingers Falls, New York: Antique Collectors' Club, 1991

Dormer, Peter, and Turner, Ralph. *The New Jewelry: Trends and Traditions.* London: Thames & Hudson, 1986

Evans, Chuck. *Jewelry: Contemporary Designs and Techniques.* Worcester, Mass.: Davis Publications, 1983

Evans, Joan. *A History of Jewelry, 1100–1870.* New York: Dover, 1989

Gabardi, Melissa. *Art Deco Jewelry.* Wappingers Falls, New York: Antique Collectors' Club, 1989

Hughes, Richard. *Colouring, Bronzing and Patination of Metals.* New York: Watson-Guptill, 1991

Mack, John, ed. *Ethnic Jewelry.* New York: Abrams, 1988

Maryon, Herbert. *Metalwork and Enamelling.* 4th edition. New York: Dover, 1971

Mascetti, Daniela, and Triossi, Amanda. *Earrings: From Antiquity to the Present.* New York: Rizzoli International, 1990

McCreight, Tim. *The Complete Metalsmith: An Illustrated Handbook.* Revised edition. Worcester, Mass.: Davis Publications, 1991

McCreight, Tim, ed. *Metals Technic, A Collection of Techniques for Metalsmiths.* Cape Elizabeth, Maine: Brynmorgen Press, 1992

McNeil, Donald S., ed. *Jewelers' Dictionary.* 3rd edition. Radnor, Penn.: Jewelers Book Club, 1979

O'Connor, Harold. *The Jeweler's Bench Reference.* Taos, New Mex.: Dunconor Books, 1978

Ogden, Jack. *Jewellery of the Ancient World.* New York: Rizzoli International, 1982

Radice, Barbara. *Jewelry by Architects.* New York: Rizzoli International, 1987

Revere, Alan. *Professional Goldsmithing: A Contemporary Guide to Traditional Jewelry Techniques.* New York: Van Nostrand Reinhold, 1991

Rodgers, Susan. *Power and Gold: Jewelry from Indonesia, Malaysia and the Philippines.* New York: TeNeues, 1988

Rose, Augustus F., and Cirino, Antonio. *Jewelry Making and Design.* New York: Dover, 1949

Ross, Heather C. *The Art of Bedouin Jewellery: A Saudi Arabian Profile.* Studio City, Calif.: Empire Publishing Service, 1990

Seitz & Finegold. *Silversmithing.* Radnor, Penn.: Chilton, 1983

Seppä, Heikki. *Form Emphasis for Metalsmiths.* Kent, Ohio: Kent State University Press, 1978

Snowman, A. Kenneth. *The Master Jewelers.* New York: Abrams, 1990

Tait, Hugh, ed. *Jewelry: Seven Thousand Years.* New York: Abrams, 1987

Untracht, Oppi. *Jewelry Concepts and Technology.* Radnor, Penn.: Jewelers Book Club, 1982
———. *Metal Techniques for Craftsmen.* New York: Doubleday, 1968

Von Neumann, Robert. *The Design and Creation of Jewelry.* 3rd edition. Radnor, Penn.: Chilton, 1982

Wicks, Sylvia. *Jewelry Making Manual.* Cape Elizabeth, Maine: Brynmorgen Press, 1985

Youngs, Susan, ed. *The Work of Angels: Masterpieces of Celtic Metalwork, 6th–9th Centuries AD.* Austin: University of Texas Press, 1989

Index